Voices on Holiness
From the Evangelical Association

by
Rev. H.J. Bowman

And they overcame him by the blood of the Lamb, and by the word of their testimony.-Rev. 12. 11.

Schmul Publishing Company
Nicholasville, Kentucky

COPYRIGHT © 2017 BY SCHMUL PUBLISHING CO.
All rights reserved. No part of this publication may be reproduced or used in any form or by any means—graphic, electronic, or mechanical, including photocopying, recording, taping, or information storage or retrieval systems—without prior written permission of the publishers.

Churches and other noncommercial interests may reproduce portions of this book without prior written permission of the publisher, provided such quotations are not offered for sale—or other compensation in any form—whether alone or as part of another publication, and provided that the text does not exceed 500 words or five percent of the entire book, whichever is less, and does not include material quoted from another publisher. When reproducing text from this book, the following credit line must be included: "From *Voices on Holiness from the Evangelical Association* by H.J. Bowman, © 2017 by Schmul Publishing Co., Nicholasville, Kentucky. Used by permission."

Cover image copyright: <a href='http://www.123rf.com/profile_almoond'>almoond / 123RF Stock Photo</a>. Used by permission.

Published by Schmul Publishing Co.
PO Box 776
Nicholasville, KY USA

Printed in the United States of America

ISBN 10: 0-88019-599-1
ISBN 13: 978-0-88019-599-7

Visit us on the Internet at www.wesleyanbooks.com, or order direct from the publisher by calling 800-772-6657, or by writing to the above address.

Contents

PUBLISHER'S PREFACE 5

PREFACE 7

INTRODUCTION 9

I THE SUBJECT PRESENTED 12

II THE VOICE OF THE CHURCH 16
    The Doctrine Stated 16
    The General Conference of A.D. 1867 20
    History and Teachings of the 22
    Article on Holiness 22
    Further Statements and Directions 42
    A Prayer for Infant Sanctification 43
    "The Doctrines of the Evangelical Association" 47
    The New Catechism 49
    Our Hymn-Book Theology on Holiness 51
    Albright, Walter and Miller 55
    Unfaithful Ministers Cannot be Sanctified 58
    The Grace of Sanctification Defined 58
    Rev. John Walter 62
    Rev. John Dreisbach 66
    Rev. Henry Fisher 68
    Bishop Seybert's Voice 79
    Bishop Joseph Long 86
    Rev. S.G. Rhoads 92
    Rev. W.W. Orwig, ... 97
    Justification, Regeneration and Sanctification 103
    Rev. Charles Hammer 105
    Rev. Jacob Schnerr 113

III   THE VOICE OF THE PRESS 115
    Sanctification—Its Condition 117
    Consecration and Faith 119
    Experimental and Practical Holiness 120
    How to Get Believers Sanctified 123
    Holiness Begun 124
    Sin in Believers 130
    Importance of Perfect Purity 135
    "Gradual and Instantaneous" 140
    Purity and Maturity 143
    Professing Holiness 146
    Two Kinds of Profession 155
    "The Holy Ones" 157
    Going on to Perfection 160
    Entire Sanctification 164
    No Heaven Without Holiness 168
    Our Sanctification Personal 170
    When We may be Sanctified 171
    The Conditions of Our Entire Sanctification 172
    Holiness a Bible Doctrine 173
    The "Holiness Movement" 177
    The Voice of the Bishops in 1879 195

IV   THE VOICE OF TESTIMONY 199
    "Ye Are My Witnesses" 199
    Experience of Rev. J. P. Leib 200
    Experience of Savilla Kring 201
    Experience of Rev. J. Bowersox 210
    Experience of Rev. H.J. Bowman 213
    Experience of Rev. W. H. Bucks 223
    Experience of Rev. H.F. Kletzing 225
    Experience of Rev. M. Krueger 228
    Experience of Rev. S. Dickover 230
    Experience of Mrs. Lizzie Yetley 232

V   CONCLUSION 234

Publisher's Preface

Soon after the Revolutionary War in America, a young veteran of the Philadelphia Militia felt the call of God on his life. Dissatisfied with Lutheranism, Jacob Albright, a descendant of German immigrants to the colony of Pennsylvania, fell in with the Methodists and was entirely sanctified.

As a native among the German community in Pennsylvania, he was able to carry the message of heart holiness among them in their own tongue. The result of his labor eventually became known as the Evangelical Association, closely following the forms and teachings of the Methodist Church, complete with its own conference structure, bishops and Book of Discipline.

This volume is a compendium of the church's teaching and beliefs concerning entire sanctification during the latter half of the nineteenth century, at the height of the Holiness Revival in America. As the spiritual pilgrimage for these Believers launched from a different embarkation point than British Methodism in England, the reader will observe slight cultural distinctions, but will also readily see the movement of the Holy Spirit in cleansing power among any who are eager to receive him.

Here is a restatement of the Second Blessing in no uncertain sound, joyfully proclaiming the Wesleyan doctrine of liberation from the guilt and power of sin.

—D. Curtis Hale
Publisher, 2017

Preface

Here is another new book for the Christian public. It is not a connected discussion of the subject of which it treats, and yet the reader will find its theme extensively discussed in a variety of ways, by the different authors whose voices here speak. Aside from the preface, the introduction, and the necessary links with which the different divisions and subjects have been connected, nothing has been expressly written for this book except a few *experiences*.

My object in making a book of this kind was to show what the views of the Evangelical Association are, as held and publicly expressed by our leading men, through all the history of our Church, and I am glad to know that a great deal more has been written and published among us in defence of holiness as a personal experience than could possibly be compressed within the limits of this volume.

In copying or quoting from these numerous writers, I have been careful to let them express their views in their own language. The translations from the German, of which I have made quite a number, may seem rather literal because of this purpose.

These Voices on Holiness were fraught with blessings to those who heard or read them as originally made public from the pulpit and by the press, and it is intended that, by means of this reproduction of them, they shall live on to encourage others to walk in the King's highway of holiness.

I don't expect every reader to approve of all that is here written, but that is no concern of mine. Having had the most satisfactory assurance, all along, of God's approval, I am content to submit to the judgment and criticisms of men.

Should, however, the reader discover any serious defects, let it be remembered that the entire work of this compilation was done in the space of about one hundred days, the compiler having at the same time performed all his ordinary duties of editing the *Living Epistle*, and the English Sunday-school periodicals of his Church.

With no pretensions but that of a plain, simple statement of God's truth, this humble volume is sent forth to bless its readers, and to glorify our exalted Redeemer.

—H.J.B.
Cleveland, O., October 21, 1882

Introduction

It was a happy thought that induced Rev. H.J. Bowman to compile the "Voices on Holiness" from the Evangelical Association, and thus unite them into one melodious harmony and marshal them before his readers in a grand chorus, rehearsing most acceptably a glorious theme. Some of these "Voices" were heard many years ago, but their authors "have gone before to the other shore," and their pens are at rest, and, hence, the present rising generation has been almost entirely deprived of their utterances. But now comes this book, and presents these precious treasures to the young, as well as the older members of the Evangelical Association, for their benefit and appreciation.

"Voices on Holiness" will be very valuable as a repertory and a book of reference, concerning what Evangelical authorities have said on the vital doctrine of holiness. It will, therefore, also be a valuable addition to the library of every preacher in this Church, and of every family in the Connection; for certainly, they all ought to acquaint themselves with what the Church says, as well as what the Bible teaches, on this subject.

This book shows clearly that the fathers and authorities of the Evangelical Association laid great stress upon the doctrine and realization of entire sanctification. They were not satisfied with the beginnings of salvation, so as to rest in them; they insisted that believers, and preachers especially, should "go on unto perfection"! Preaching Christ, they taught emphatically that he is made unto us *sanctification* as well as wisdom, righteousness, and redemption, and in this they proved themselves excellent practical theologians. And their work was, also in this respect, abundantly owned and blessed by the Great Master.

The attentive reader of this volume will find that sanctification or holiness is viewed chiefly in its experimental and practical aspects, or in other words as *inward* and *outward* and hence *personal holiness*. This is highly Scriptural. Neither the Bible nor our Church recognizes an *antinomian* holiness, that consists in theory and formal profession only while the person remains unholy; nor do they teach that we are holy in Christ by construction, or a sort of an "imputation," while impure in ourselves; but they insist that *we* should be holy. "*Be ye* holy, for I am holy" says the Holy One of Israel. And this holiness pertains to "all the heart," and "all manner of conversation," —("living" says the Revision) in a word to the *whole inward and outward life*.

But while insisting earnestly on subjective, practical holiness we must ever remember that all true holiness must and can only come by faith from the objective source: the glorified Lord and Saviour Jesus Christ. As branches are fully and uninterruptedly united with the vine, and are thus filled with life and sap which produces abundant fruit, so we must be united spiritually with the "True Vine." Thus abiding in Him, he will abide in us, and we shall bring forth much fruit to the glory of the Father (John 15). Then "Christ is our life," "Christ in us the hope of glory." He then keeps pure and invigorates the inner man, from which results, certainly, an outward holy life. This prevents, on the one hand, a mere outward pharisaic sanctimoniousness, and, on the other hand, one-sided, selfish fanaticism. Christ before us, as the pattern, and Christ in us, as the life and controlling power, will be a perfect regulator, and make holiness *entire* and *symmetrical*.—And to Him will be given all the glory in our life and confession. "That according as it is written: He that glorieth, let him glory in the Lord."

"And the very God of peace sanctify you wholly; and I pray God your whole spirit, soul, and body be preserved blameless unto the coming of our Lord Jesus Christ. Faithful is he that calleth you who also will do it." (2 Thess. 5. 23, 24.)

—R.Y.
Naperville, Ill., Oct. 10, 1882

I
THE SUBJECT PRESENTED

THERE CAME A TIME in the history of the Christian religion, when the Church and the world were very much alike,—not because the Church had converted the world, but because she had compromised with it. The spirit of worldliness prevailed to an alarming extent throughout the various religious denominations. There was but little religious power or real Christian activity; and genuine conversions, followed with holy living, were rare. The fewest of those that constituted the membership of the Churches lived a life of separation from the world, and of Scriptural cross-bearing. Christian testimony was dying out,—especially that bold witnessing for Christ which was formerly heard from the lips of those upon whom the Holy Ghost had come. The blessed truths of the Gospel were mostly held *in theory only*, and *experience* was quite unpopular,—especially the experience of any very high degree of spiritual life.

Holiness, the "Central Idea of Christianity," was almost entirely ignored as an actual personal experience, and "religious culture" was substituted for a vigorous Gospel faith, and a well-defined Christian experience.

As a result there was but little "fruit unto holiness," and much unholy ambition, and self-seeking, both among the ministry and the laity.

In their rivalry for the finest and most fashionable church buildings, and the most cultured and popular ministry, the Churches were fast losing sight of the Crucified One, and of the perishing poor to whom the Gospel was ordained to be preached.

Then there came a time, when great efforts were made to bring about a revival of Primitive Christianity. The Churches began to wake up, and in course of a few years there was great commotion in many places among the believers in Christ.

From many pulpits came appeals to the Church to awake, and put on her strength and her beautiful garments—to arise to a "higher life"—to "go on to perfection"—to be "wholly sanctified."—From the prayer and class-room went forth exhortations to believers to seek full salvation. From pulpit and pew came the voice of testimony, crying: "The blood cleanseth us from all sin."

Through the press these doctrines, exhortations, and testimonies were scattered broadcast over the land, and special meetings sprang up all over the country to consider these matters, and get the people to fall in line and strive for the experience of entire sanctification, and the "promotion of Scriptural holiness."

This aggressive movement created a stir in the valley of dry bones,—the worldly, formal, dead Churches—and great fears were expressed that the agitators of the holiness question would spread fanaticism, and "split the Church." Then I became anxious to hear some voice that would give "a certain sound" on this great theme—a voice whose authority all would be bound to respect.

So I turned to the Bible for *the voice of God*, and instantly my ear caught such utterances as these: "Be ye holy; for I am holy." 1 Pet. 1. 16.—"This is the will of God, even your sanctification." 1 Thess. 4. 3.—"Christ loved the Church, and gave himself for it; that he might sanctify and cleanse it with the washing of water by the word, that he might present it to himself a glorious Church, not having spot or wrinkle, or any such thing; but that it should be holy and without blemish." Eph. 5. 25-27.— "Be ye therefore perfect, even as your Father which is in heaven is perfect." Matt. 5. 48.—"Therefore, leaving the principles of the doctrine of Christ, let us go on unto perfection." Heb. 6. 1.—"Then will I sprinkle clean water upon you, and ye shall be clean: from all your filthiness, and from all your idols, will I cleanse you. A new heart also will I give you, and a new spirit will I put within you; and I will take away the stony heart out of your flesh. And I will put my spirit within you, and cause you to walk in my statutes, and ye shall keep my judgments, and do them." Ezek. 36. 25-27.—"Having therefore these promises, dearly beloved, let us cleanse ourselves from all filthiness of the flesh and spirit, perfecting holiness in the fear of God." 2 Cor. 7. 1. "If we walk in the light, as he is in the light, we have fellowship one with another, and the blood of Jesus Christ his Son cleanseth us from all sin." 1 John 1. 7.—"And the very God of peace sanctify you wholly; and I pray God your whole spirit and soul and body be preserved blameless unto the coming of our Lord Jesus Christ. Faithful is he that calleth you, who also will do it." 1 Thess. 5. 23, 24.—"But the God of all grace, who hath called us unto his eternal glory by Christ Jesus, after that ye have suffered a while, make you perfect, stablish, strengthen, settle you." 1 Pet. 5. 10.—"But ye shall receive power, after that the Holy Ghost is come upon you; and ye shall be witnesses unto me both in Jerusalem, and in all Judea and in Samaria, and unto the uttermost part of the earth." Acts 1. 8.

Thus the voice of inspiration kept pouring volumes of thought into my mind about holiness, which plainly showed me that it was both the duty and the privilege of every believer to be made pure from all moral defilement, perfect in love, full of the Spirit, and a *living* witness to the *fullness* of the blessings of the Gospel of Christ.

II
THE VOICE OF THE CHURCH

Having heard the voice of God, I next turned to hear how this great Bible subject was presented through the voice of the Church.

THE DOCTRINE STATED

Presently I heard a statement, which came from her Book of Discipline. And, from the many voices here joined in unison, from several generations past, as well as from the present, it seemed to be given with indisputable authority. And these are the things that I heard:—

THE DOCTRINE OF CHRISTIAN PERFECTION
HOW WE MAY ATTAIN TO TRUE HOLINESS OF HEART EVEN IN THIS LIFE

The Lord Jesus expressly says, Matt. 5. 48, *Be ye therefore perfect, even as your Father which is in heaven is perfect.* And the Apostle Paul exhorts, 1 Thess. 5. 16-18, *Rejoice evermore; pray without ceasing; in everything give thanks; for this is the will of God in Christ Jesus concerning you.*

He that would fully comply with these exhortations at all times, must be wholly resigned to the will of God; consequently all self-will and selfishness must be perfectly subdued; he must bear everything that may befall him, as from the hand of the Lord, or he cannot meet every adversity with acquiescence and resignation, much less with gratitude. He must stand upon his guard so firmly and immovably that he can parry, and gain the victory over any temptation the moment that it may present itself, without yielding more or less, either voluntarily or negligently, as it does sometimes happen with weak Christians. If his rest, peace, and joy in God, are no more interrupted by any such vicissitudes or occurrences, he must indeed be firmly rooted and grounded in God; and of a truth, he must love God with all his heart, with all his mind, and with all his strength; sin has, as it were, lost all its power against such a one, he being surrounded by the love of God, as with a wall of fire. The flesh, the world, and Satan, are under his feet, and he rules over his enemies, yet in watchfulness.

This is the state which the Evangelical Association understands by CHRISTIAN PERFECTION.

That such a state is attainable, even in this life, is very evident, for Christ and all his apostles exhort thereto; yea, from this we learn that it is every Christian's bounden duty to strive thereafter. And how can he be a Christian, who does not desire to submit wholly to God, and to love him in truth, with all his heart, with all his soul, and with all his strength?

By experience we are fully persuaded that such a state is attainable, and has been attained by many, who have happily persevered therein for many years, even to the end of their days. Many others had attained it, but for want of watchfulness lost it again. This we also have learned by sad experience. But experience has likewise taught that this blessed state, after it has been lost through negligence, may again be attained by the grace of God, and that a person may finally, after having been as a reed shaken by the wind, become as a firm and immovable pillar in the temple of God.

With many others this work has never come to a perfect clearness; a great degree of grace was indeed visible, yet there were also infirmities discernible at the same time, which could not be properly distinguished by those who look upon externals only, whether they were but involuntary, natural infirmities, or slighter voluntary deviations and overcomings of sin.

Experience has moreover taught that, ordinarily, this state of Christian perfection is attained gradually, by an upright course of life in following the Lamb; however, during this gradation, this work is perfected in the soul, sooner or later, by a sudden and powerful influence of grace and outpouring of the Divine Spirit. Those who have actually experienced it describe this effusion of the divine life as being similar to the grace of justification, yet far exceeding the same. This grace is called SANCTIFICATION.

This sanctification is the basis of Christian perfection. By it God writes his law of love with quickening power into the heart, according to his precious and faithful promises.

Notwithstanding, as all created beings will ever remain finite and circumscribed, and, according to the nature thereof, are forever less than God himself; the most perfect man (or angel) will ever be inferior to God, though he become a partaker of the Divine nature by justification, and through sanctification be much more assimilated to the Divine Being: therefore he may, after having attained to this degree of sanctification, grow and increase yet more and more in grace, and proceed from one degree of glory to another.

And where this progression should cease cannot be conceived; rather may we suppose a continual advancement and progression to all eternity. Nevertheless, the happiest spirit will ever remain greatly inferior to God himself.

It is further to be considered here, that sanctifying grace does not take away the natural infirmities of man, yea, it does not even cover them; but, on the other hand, it sometimes rather manifests and exposes them. Such are, a weakly and morbid body, weakness of understanding, of memory, of judgment, and of the mind. Therefore such an individual may be imposed upon by false appearances, and through a misdirected judgment think more highly or derogatively of other persons than they really deserve. He may be indistinct, yea, confused in expression; give unfit advice; and through various kinds of such weaknesses, which God never imputes as sins, he may render himself ridiculous before a witty world. Such a one should, therefore, never refuse to receive instruction and good counsel from others who do not possess the same degree of grace with him, as far as he sees that God designs to instruct him in this.

This much has been deemed necessary to be stated here, to prevent all misunderstanding of the matter, and to enable the reader to see this doctrine in a clear light, and to form just conceptions thereof. Whereupon the Evangelical Association further declares:

Let us, then, seriously and explicitly admonish all believers, ardently to strive for Christian perfection. And in order that we may teach uniformly on this point, let us decide, once for all, whether we shall continue or give up this doctrine. We are unanimous to defend and maintain it; understanding by it nothing else than a total deliverance from all sin in the proper sense of the word, by means of the love of God being shed abroad in the heart influencing and actuating the same.

Some indeed say: "This cannot be attained, till we have passed through purgatory." Others say: "No, this is accomplished at the moment when body and soul are separated." Again, others say: "We can attain this before we die, one minute afterward is too late." But we are unanimous that we may be redeemed from all sin long before we die; that is, from all evil affections and desires. So this point remains settled.

The next inquiry is: Is this happy change wrought gradually or instantaneously? Both take place. Shall we, then, insist upon one as well as the other, in our preaching? We must certainly insist upon a gradual change, and this zealously and continually. And have we not equally as good reasons to insist upon an instantaneous change, wrought by the effusion of grace in an instant? If we can expect such a blessed change, should we not earnestly exhort all believers to seek it? And the more so, because the more earnestly this instantaneous work of grace is sought, the more it is longed for, the more rapidly and steadfastly the gradual work of grace in the soul will progress. The more they are concerned about such a change, the more punctual will they be in observing the divine ordinances: whereas, on the other hand, the contrary may be observed in all those who are not expecting this work of grace. They are blessed in the hope and expectation of a total change, while gradually growing in grace. But where this hope falls away, the work of grace begins to stagnate, if it does not apparently decrease. Therefore, whosoever is concerned to promote the gradual progress of this work, should encourage believers in the hope of such an immediate influence of grace. So far the Discipline.

After this she gave forth her voice again through a unanimous vote of

The General Conference of A.D. 1867,

which was passed with such an emphasis that it might well have silenced all differences. It was in view of certain diverging opinions concerning the doctrine of Christian Perfection that this matter was brought before this General Conference, then assembled at Pittsburgh, Pa., for adjustment.

A committee was appointed to prepare a statement representing the views of the Conference, which committee consisted of two bishops, and one delegate from each annual conference. The names of the committee are: Bishop J. Long, Bishop J. J. Esher, Reverends F. Hoffman, E. Kohr, T. G. Clewell, D. Fisher, H. Rohland, H. Huelster, John Dreisbach, W. Smith, M. Krueger, M. J. Miller, H. Lageschulte and J. F. Schreiber.

After due deliberation the following was reported, and unanimously adopted by a rising vote:

> Your committee desires to submit the following as their unanimous report on the doctrine of Sanctification:
>
> As for some time past different opinions and views of the doctrine of Sanctification and Christian Perfection have been advanced among us, and as this state of things threatens harm in various ways, therefore,
>
> Resolved, That we are still convinced as we have hitherto been, of the Scripturalness of the doctrine of Sanctification and Christian Perfection as contained in our book of Discipline, and delivered unto us by the fathers of our Church, unanimously declare that we, as we have hitherto done, shall also in future, hold to, teach and defend the following points:
>
> 1. Our Lord and Saviour Jesus Christ is the only but all-sufficient Source (cause), and the perfect pattern of our Sanctification and Christian Perfection.
>
> 2. Entire Sanctification has its foundation in regeneration, and consists in a complete consecration to God and salvation from all sin, i. e., all evil affections and desires, together with the enjoyment of the perfect love of God wrought by the Holy Ghost, and Christ dwelling in us, whose blood cleanseth from all sin.
>
> 3. Christian Perfection consists in this, that we at all times and under all circumstances love God with all our hearts, our neighbors as ourselves, and God's children affectionately, and thus have the mind that was in Christ, and walk even as he walked.
>
> 4. That this state of Sanctification and Christian Perfection is attainable in this life, yea, long before death,

and may be retained unimpaired, by watchfulness and faithfulness, even unto the end, with a continual growth in grace, and progress from glory unto glory.

5. That this state is obtained by an entire consecration and offering of ourselves to God, and faith in our Lord Jesus Christ; these being the only conditions taught and laid down in the word of God— usually by a gradual progress, but often also instantaneously, in proportion as our consecration is complete, and our faith in Christ is strong, excluding all doubt.

Resolved, further, That we most earnestly advise all our preachers that they, in all their public teachings and sermons, as well as private instruction on this all-important subject, carefully and deliberately use such terms and phrases as cannot be misunderstood, nor lead to deviations from the clearly expressed sense of our doctrine, so that uniformity of opinion may prevail among us, and we, as nearly as possible, use one mode of expression.

The minutes of the Conference add the following: "An inquiry was here presented as to what is to be thought of the so-called *holiness meetings*, and whether they ought to be encouraged or suppressed; "to which Bishop Long, then in the chair, remarked: "I should think if such meetings are held in the fear of God, for the purpose of seeking and promoting Sanctification, we ought to rejoice and cooperate with them, but if they degenerate, the contrary ought to be done."

History and Teachings of the Article on Holiness

In A.D. 1876, Rev. R. Yeakel, then one of the Bishops of the Evangelical Association, published a series of articles in the *Evangelical Messenger*, in which he set forth the History, Theology, Experimental Teachings, and Practical Directions of the Article on Christian Perfection in the following manner: —

I. Its History

Among the Articles of Faith, Doctrines, Directions and Rules contained in the Discipline of the Evangelical Association, the Article on "Christian Perfection," teaching "how we may attain to true holiness of heart even in this life," occupies a prominent place, and with regard to Christian experience and practice it stands preeminent. From the fact that every minister in our connection is required to preach the doctrines it contains, and every member enjoined to seek the state of grace it describes, it is all-important.

We may as well confess the truth at once that there exists both among our ministry and laity, a great lack of correct information, amounting in not a few cases to a total ignorance of the origin and history of this article, and to some extent of the true import of its teachings and directions.

It has been said by some that the fathers of our Church composed this article and inserted it into our Discipline as an *essay* on the subject. Others have thought that some leading man put it into the Discipline at a later time, and that, consequently, it did not belong to the fundamentals of our doctrines. Some have thought that it was not *Wesleyan*, hence not to be construed according to the well-known teachings of that eminent man of God, etc. Avoiding at this juncture all discussion of these opinions, we will endeavor to present the history, theology, experimental teachings, and practical directions of this excellent Article, for the sole purpose of throwing light upon it, and inciting the reader to a careful and prayerful perusal and study of this part of our doctrines, in the light of the holy Scriptures and experimental truth.

The Article has a history and a development, and to understand the same correctly, we must ascertain and study this history. Both the Old and New Testaments begin with history, and he who would know the doctrines of the Bible correctly, needs to begin with these; for theology is not only eternal truth, but it is largely based upon the facts of Scripture history. "All false philosophies begin somewhere in the middle," says a wise man. Let us avoid this error, and begin at the beginning and tread upon solid ground.

The historical beginnings of our Article constitute a part of the history of Methodism in England and America, hence we introduce as much of it here as may be necessary for our purpose.

The Methodist societies were originally governed by General Rules drawn up by the Wesleys, in 1743, and by the regulations adopted in the conferences which were held yearly from 1744. These regulations were first published in the so-called "Minutes" from year to year. They were afterwards collected and printed in a tract usually called "The Large Minutes," the title of which reads thus: "Minutes of several conversations between Rev. Mr. Wesley and others, from the year 1744 to the year 1789." These rules and regulations governed the Methodist societies in America to some extent, from the time of their formation in 1766. At successive conferences additional regulations were adopted until the year 1784, when, peace having been concluded between England and the United States, and the independence of the latter acknowledged, the Methodist societies here were formed into the "Methodist Episcopal Church" and their first Discipline published, under the following remarkable title: "Minutes of several conversations between the Rev. Thomas Coke, LL.D., the Rev. Francis Asbury, and others, at a conference begun in Baltimore, in the State of Maryland, on Monday, the 27th of December, in the year 1784. Composing a form of Discipline for the ministers, preachers, and other members of the Methodist Episcopal Church in America."

These "Large Minutes" of Wesley's conferences, and the

first Discipline of the M.E. Church, contain the main part of our Article in the form of an answer to the question, "What can be done in order to revive the work of God where it is decayed?" as follows:

> "Strongly and explicitly exhort all believers to 'go on unto perfection.' That we may 'all speak the same thing,' we ask, once for all, Shall we defend this perfection, or give it up? We all agree to defend it, meaning thereby (as we did from the beginning,) salvation from all sin, by the love of God and man filling our heart. The Papists say, 'This cannot be attained till we have been refined by the fire of purgatory.' The Calvinists say, 'Nay, it will be attained as soon as soul and body part.' The old Methodists say, 'It may be attained before we die, a moment after is too late.' Is it so or not? We are all agreed we may be saved from all sin before death. The substance then is settled; but, as to circumstance, is the change gradual or instantaneous? It is both the one and the other."

The "Large Minutes" contained the following paragraph in immediate succession to the above, which was left out of the M.E. Discipline of 1784:

> "From the moment we are justified, there may be a gradual sanctification, a growing in grace, a daily advance in the knowledge and love of God. And if sin cease before death, there must, in the nature of the thing, be an instantaneous change; there must be a last moment wherein it does exist, and a first moment wherein it does not."

Then the article proceeds:

> "'But should we in preaching insist both on one and the other?' Certainly we must insist on the gradual change, and that earnestly and continually. And are

there not reasons why we should insist on the instantaneous also? If there be such a blessed change before death, should we not encourage all believers to expect it? And the rather, because constant experience shows, the more earnestly they expect this, the more swiftly and steadily does the gradual work of God go on in their souls; the more watchful they are against all sin, the more careful to grow in grace, the more zealous of good works, and the more punctual in their attendance on all the ordinances of God. Whereas just the contrary effects are observed whenever this expectation ceases. They are 'saved by hope,' by this hope of a total change, with a gradually increasing salvation. Destroy this hope, and that salvation stands still, or rather, decreases daily. Therefore whoever would advance the gradual change in believers, should strongly insist on the instantaneous."

From the foregoing we see that the *origin* of our Article dates back to the conferences or "conversations between the Rev. Mr. Wesley and others, from the year 1744 to the year 1789." Whoever acquaints himself with the life of Wesley and the history of Methodism during his life, will find that a large portion of their conference business consisted of "conversations" or *discussions* of doctrines and their settlement into what may be properly called Methodist Theology, under the supervision and direction of Mr. Wesley; and among these doctrines was the "Doctrine of Christian Perfection. How we may attain to true holiness of heart, even in this life." which we now have in our Discipline.

It is true the original article in the "Large Minutes" and the first M.E. Discipline contains a few verbal variations, and also lacks a few paragraphs of the first part of the Article as it now stands in our book, but these were afterwards supplied from Mr. Wesley's writings.

Our Article in the Discipline is, historically considered, altogether and thoroughly *Wesleyan*.

We have noticed the embryonic beginning and the development of this Article during the early history of Wesleyan Methodism, and how it appeared finally in the first M.E. Discipline of 1784. We next find it enriched and enlarged from the writings of Wesley to its present size and thus appear in the Methodist Discipline up to 1812. It was then omitted from their Discipline, with other doctrinal writings, and printed separately.

God, in his wondrous ways, choosing "the weak things of the world to confound things that are mighty," awakened, converted and called into the Gospel ministry Rev. Jacob Albright, who became, under providential guidance, the founder of the Evangelical Association. His object was to preach repentance, faith and holiness to the neglected Pennsylvania Germans, of whom he himself was one. His labors from 1795 to 1800 were blessed so far that a little flock of earnest souls gathered around him and organized the Evangelical Association in 1800.

Mr. Albright having joined the M.E. Church after his conversion, before he commenced preaching, from a preference for their excellent Church Discipline, which was at that time pretty faithfully administered, labored afterward doctrinally and otherwise after the Methodistic pattern, and after the Evangelical Association had been organized, the necessity of a book of Discipline, containing the doctrines and rules of the Church, was felt and discussed. Finally, in 1807, it was concluded that Albright should compile such a work. But the messenger of death came and led him over Jordan into the glorious rest that remaineth for the people of God, on the 18th of May, 1808, before he could accomplish the compilation of the Discipline.

This work was then entrusted to Rev. George Miller, who published it in 1809.

In the year 1808, Rev. Henry Boehm, a minister of the

M.E. Church, translated the entire M.E. Discipline, as it had been issued in 1804, into German, and had it printed at Lancaster, Pa. A copy of this issue is before me. It contains the Article on Christian Perfection as it now stands in our German Discipline, verbatim. This Discipline was the text-book from which our Discipline was prepared, which G. Miller published the following year. A copy of this, our first edition, also lies before me. A comparison of the two shows that the article on Christian Perfection was transferred from the German M.E. Discipline into that of the Evangelical Association, and thus the Wesleyan Methodist doctrine of Sanctification or Perfection introduced and adopted fundamentally as one of the doctrines of the Evangelical Association.

Mr. Albright preached this doctrine very often, and inculcated the necessity of seeking entire sanctification in his conversations with his co-laborers, and also among the members, according to the testimony of Rev. Geo. Miller, in his autobiography, and of Rev. John Dreisbach, as given to the writer. There is no doubt whatever that if Albright had lived long enough to complete the Discipline, he would have introduced the same Article as an exposition of the doctrine held by our Church, for he was thoroughly Methodistic in his doctrinal views.

Thus, then, we see that the German version of the Article is in our Church the original one. It remained the only one until the General Conference of 1830 appointed a committee, consisting of A. Ettinger and John Dreisbach, on the translation of the Discipline into the English language.

At that General Conference great changes were made in the Discipline. Among others, several doctrinal sections, as for instance, on Predestination, Antinomianism and Perseverance, which were somewhat polemical, were omitted, but the Article on Perfection was retained, it being the "established and standing doctrine from the beginning on this subject," as Father Dreisbach expressed it.

During later years a few men among us attempted to introduce views into the Church differing from those contained in the Article, which resulted in the *unanimous* declaration of the General Conference, held in Pittsburgh, Pa., in the year 1867, that we now and in the future hold fast to the doctrine as delivered unto us by the fathers in the Book of Discipline. It is also worthy of note that, previous to this General Conference, a revision of the form of the Article failed of getting a sufficient number of votes from the annual conferences to carry it before General Conference for action.

The General Conference of 1871 ordered that the article be placed immediately after the Articles of Faith in the Discipline, that being considered its most appropriate place in the book.

In closing this historical sketch we remark,

1. That the Article is altogether Wesleyan.

2. That it was incorporated into our Church Discipline from the beginning, and is the only and *fundamental* doctrine of the Evangelical Association on this subject.

3. That the German version is the original one among us.

4. That when the Discipline was greatly changed in 1830 this Article remained unaltered.

5. That a recommendation for a change even of its systematic arrangement, was refused by the annual conferences, and General Conference again unanimously confirmed it by the adoption of confirmatory and expository resolutions.

6. That no other part of our Discipline has passed through more sifting discussions for so many years, and remained so entirely untouched during all the frequent alterations of *all its other* parts.

7. That no other portion of our book has so often "been confirmed during our history, nor occupies so large a space in our Discipline.

II. Its Theology

We have seen from its history that the Article is thoroughly Wesleyan. From this it is evident that its theology is also Wesleyan.

What does it teach theologically?

1. It teaches a state of Christian experience and of Divine grace, called Sanctification and Christian Perfection. It teaches this from the Scriptures,— from Matt. 5. 48, "*Be ye therefore perfect, even as your Father which is in heaven is perfect;*" and 1 Thess. 5. 16-18. It describes this as a state in which the Christian is "wholly resigned to the will of God," and "consequently all self-will and selfishness must be perfectly subdued." "He loves God with all his heart, with all his mind, and with all his strength." "Sin has lost, as it were, all its power against such a one, he being surrounded by the love of God, as with a wall of fire. The flesh, the world, and Satan are under his feet, and he rules over his enemies; yet watching and not slumbering. This is the state which the Evangelical Association understands by Christian Perfection."

We have quoted only the positive statements or definitions of this portion; that which is negative and circumstantial will be noticed hereafter. There is no apparent reason for any discussion of this doctrine *per se*, as the Bible is full of it.

2. It teaches that this state of grace is not attained at the new birth, by saying: "Let us, then, seriously and explicitly admonish all believers ardently to strive for Christian Perfection." And this fully accords with what the Scriptures enjoin upon believers: "Let us go on unto perfection." Although there is a certain kind of perfection belonging to babes in Christ, yet it is not that of which the Scriptures speak. They distinguish perfection just as much as manhood is distinct from childhood. Every Bible reader knows this to be so.

3. It teaches that this state of grace can be reached "long before we die." This is Scriptural. *Christ* "saves to the uttermost." Death is no Saviour in any sense, and does not change our moral condition in the least. He is an enemy that shall be made Christ's footstool. *"Now* is the day of salvation." "By grace ye are saved, through faith." Then why not now?

4. It teaches that this Perfection includes salvation from all sin. "And in order that we may teach one and the same thing on this point, let us decide, once for all, whether we shall continue or give up this doctrine. We are all unanimous to defend and maintain it, understanding by it now, as at all times before, nothing more than a total deliverance from all sin, in the proper sense of the word, by means of the love of God being shed abroad in our heart, influencing and actuating the same." "We are unanimous that we may be redeemed from all sin long before we die, that is, from all evil affections and desires. Thus the main point remains settled."

This full salvation *"from all sin"* after conversion, but long before we die, is, then, the *main point* settled.

Thus the Article unequivocally teaches "sin in believers" previous to the attainment of Christian Perfection, which sin is defined as consisting of "evil desires and affections." It is not *actual* sin, either of commission or omission, nor is it the sin of the backslider that is here spoken of. The believer has already, according to the Article, obtained the "grace of justification" and by it "becomes a partaker of the divine nature." And, as John says, such a one "cannot sin, for his seed remaineth in him."

What this Article means by "all sin" is set forth so clearly by Mr. Wesley in his sermon "On sin in believers," that any sensible reader will at once perceive what is meant by this phrase. Says he: "By sin, I here understand inward sin; any sinful temper, passion, or affection; such as pride, self-will, love of the world, in any kind or degree; such as lust, anger, peevishness; any disposition contrary to the mind which was in Christ. The question is not concerning *outward sin*; whether a child of God *commit sin* or not. We all agree and earnestly maintain, "He that committeth sin is of the devil." We agree, "Whosoever is born of God does not commit sin," etc.

The phrase "from all sin" does evidently not mean that "*all* sin" which is in the unregenerate heart has remained in the believer, for Wesley says in the same sermon, "We allow that the state of a justified person is inexpressibly great and glorious. He is born again, 'not of blood, nor of flesh, nor of the will of man, but of God.' He is a child of God, a member of Christ, an heir of the kingdom of heaven. 'The peace of God which passeth all understanding, keepeth his heart and mind in Christ Jesus.' His very body is a temple of the Holy Ghost and a habitation of God through the Spirit. He is created anew in Christ Jesus, he is *washed*, he is sanctified."

Does any one say, "To teach that justified persons are not saved from all sin, and yet that they are washed and sanctified is a contradiction and therefore an error"? Paul says the same things of those whom he calls brethren. He says, "They are sanctified in Christ Jesus," they "are washed" and "sanctified," but still they "are yet carnal," and he exhorts them to "cleanse themselves from all filthiness of the flesh and spirit, *perfecting holiness* in the fear of God." There are many things in heaven and in nature, and in the depth of the human soul, that neither mathematics, nor logic, nor metaphysics can measure or reconcile, and yet they are true. The fact is that the universal experience of faithful Christians during all ages corroborates, the testimony of God's Word. Who can stand up and say that since his conversion no evil desire, no self-will, selfishness, or any evil passion ever stirred within? And this sometimes in the midst of the holiest exercises, as well as during trials.

"But are these *sin*?" They are remains of original or inbred sin. To deny that this is sin is derogatory to the law of God. "By the law is the knowledge of sin"—what it is, and how far it extends. "Sin is the transgression of the law." Now the law is *spiritual*," says the Bible; its reference to outward acts is secondary. Its requirement is that the *spiritual state* of man—the moral nature of his spiritual powers—be altogether holy at all times; and this just as much when man is physically asleep and inactive, as when he is wide awake and doing. The summary command, "Thou shalt love the Lord thy God with all thy heart, soul, mind and strength," which describes a spiritual *state*, is the *primary requirement* of the law—it is the essence of it—for "love is the fulfilling of the law." Whatsoever opposes this law in the least degree is sin. Any state of heart where evil desires are not altogether absent, and the love of God controlling and permeating the whole man, is partially sinful. A state of heart that does not comport always and fully with this law, is, *in so far*, a transgression of the law, because of its non-conformity to it.

The exceedingly superficial Pelagian view that sin is only a special act, or a series of acts, is not found in the Bible nor in this Article. Sin in man is primarily a depraved state, and as such a unit, and evil *acts* are but its outbreaking fruits.

When it is said that in "conversion all our sins are forgiven," it is expressing what belongs to justification. Actual sins, that burdened the conscience with guilt, are all forgiven, and their punishment taken away by Christ; but when such a phrase is used to deny the need of cleansing from the remains of inbred sin, it indicates a great confusion of ideas. There is nothing to pardon in sanctification, but to cleanse and "*sanctify wholly*" and thus complete that sanctification which was begun foundationally in regeneration.

In this Article the term "SANCTIFICATION," printed in capital letters by way of eminence—is used to express the instantaneously completed work of sanctification, in its negative sense, meaning the deliverance from all sin. This is stated thus: "This work is perfected in the soul, sooner or later, by a sudden and powerful influence of grace and outpouring of the Divine Spirit. Those who have actually experienced it, describe this effusion of the Divine life as being similar to the grace of justification, yet far exceeding the same. This grace is therefore called SANCTIFICATION."

"*This grace*" just described as completing salvation from all sin, is sanctification in a preeminent sense, inclusive of all that has been wrought in that direction in regeneration and during an "upright course in following the Lamb." The adjective "entire." though not incorrect, which is so frequently used at the present time, is not found in the Article at all.

It may be well to remark that the term "justification" is also used in this Article as inclusive of all that precedes justification, and what is inseparably consequent upon it, viz., regeneration, and is called "the grace of justification," stating that a Christian has "become a partaker of the Divine nature by *justification*, and by *sanctification* he is much more assimilated to the Divine Being." The two terms are comprehensive, and describe inclusively and definitely two states, or degrees of Christian experience. Paul used the term "justified" in the same inclusive and preeminent sense, and it is therefore both Scriptural and Evangelical to speak of the "*justified*" Sometimes the Scriptures also speak of those entirely sanctified, as the "sanctified," the same is true with reference to this term.

The Article teaches that "this sanctification is the basis of Christian Perfection." I always had a special liking for this sentence, because it is so much in place. As repentance is in the order of experience the basis of faith, and faith the basis of justification, and justification that of regeneration and, finally, the resurrection that of glorification, so is sanctification in its negative sense, meaning the destruction of all sin or purification from all moral depravity, the basis of Christian Perfection. Sin being all removed, and the love of God perfected, now the life of Christian Perfection begins immediately (which is also holiness *positively* considered), and includes the becoming filled with all the fulness of God, which shall never end. "Therefore he may, after having attained to this degree of sanctification, grow and increase yet more and more in grace, and proceed from one degree of glory to another. And where this progression should be brought to a point, is not to be conceived; rather may we suppose a continual advancement and progression to all eternity."

This sanctification is also termed "a change." It is not a change of grace, nor of means, nor of anything but concerning that which is under immediate consideration, viz., deliverance from all sin and being *filled* with the love of God. Inasmuch as sin is thereby all removed and the love of God in us made perfect, there is a real change to that extent and in that respect. And it is a great change. And from this fact the subsequent life of Christian Perfection is fitly called "this state." This Article is very precise in using definite pronouns and articles in describing "*this* work" and "*the* state," which shows plainly that there is a prominent distinctness, definiteness and specialty about this sanctification that distinguishes it from the "grace of justification;" but there is nothing to be found that indicates a separateness. On the contrary it teaches directly and indirectly that there is an inherent connection and progression, even from the beginnings of grace, into the depths of a glorious eternity.

The above mentioned change is predicated upon the instantaneous work, and also upon that growth in grace, which precedes it and is in respect to the latter termed a "gradual change." As the word "change" has reference to salvation from all sin, we see plainly that the Article, when speaking of a "gradual change," means gradual salvation from all sin. Hence it teaches that as grace increases sin diminishes until it is ended by the instantaneous completion of the work. The view that a Christian may, previous to entire SANCTIFICATION, grow in grace, and yet sin not decrease thereby, is not in this Article. There is a gradual *"change"* until it is *completed instantaneously.*

The Article teaches further, that this Sanctification and the consequent life of Christian Perfection does not extend further than our *moral* nature. It is not the *"glorification* of our persons," it is simply salvation "from all sin," from all those "evil desires and affections" that are contrary to the law of love. By the removal of all that is evil, "God writes his law of love with quickening power in the heart, according to his precious and faithful promises," so as "to love him in truth with all his heart, with all his soul, and with all his strength." Thus the Christian's *love* is made perfect, not his body, nor his intellect, nor his memory. This perfection of love excludes all that opposes God; it does not, however, preclude the further increase in this love. "Notwithstanding, as all created beings will ever remain finite and circumscribed, and according to the nature thereof, are at all times and forever less than God himself; the most perfect man or angel will forever be inferior to God, though he become a partaker of the Divine nature by justification, and through sanctification be much more assimilated to the Divine Being, he may after having attained to this degree of sanctification, grow and increase yet more and more in grace, and proceed from one degree of glory to another. And where this progression should be brought to a point, is not to be conceived; rather may we suppose a continual advancement and progression to all eternity."

From this it is very evident that our Article does in no wise teach an angelic, nor an Adamic, much less an absolute perfection. "Sanctifying grace does not take away the natural infirmities of man, yea it does not even cover them, but, on the other hand, sometimes manifests and exposes them more. Such are a weakly and morbid body, weakness of understanding, of memory, of judgment and of mind. Therefore such an individual may be imposed upon by false appearances, and, through a misdirected judgment, think more highly or derogatively of other persons than they really deserve, be indistinct, yea, confused in expression, give unfit advice, and through all kinds of such weaknesses, which God never beholds or imputes as wilful sins, he may render himself exceptional and ridiculous before a witty world."

The "sanctified" or perfect Christian, then, will not only grow and increase in grace and love, but he has a great work to do in improving, training and correcting his mental powers, and perfecting his words and actions. The "spots" and "filthiness" are all washed out by the blood of the Lamb, but the "wrinkles" above indicated are yet to be removed. No one will see more clearly these frailties and shortcomings than the perfect Christian himself, because he walks closely with God and in his light discovers a thousand infirmities in and about himself, of which others perhaps make no account; and although God does not impute them as sin, yet he is humbled thereby and longs the more for that future heavenly perfection by which all that is "in part" will be done away, and he "shall be like Him" who is not only "spotless" but also *faultless*. He will, therefore, thankfully accept the following admonition: "Such a one should, therefore, never refuse to receive instruction and good counsel from others, who do not possess the same degree of grace with him, as far as he sees that God designs to instruct him in this way."

III. Its Experimental Teachings

Mr. Wesley was a very close observer of men and things, and an astute reasoner. He incorporated his observations of the experience of sanctification into this Article, together with some logical conclusions therefrom. As the Bible is not a book given to relate Christian experience, but leaves it to be wrought out by the Holy Ghost, who worketh in believers according to his good pleasure, Wesley's method of ascertaining the circumstances and details of "this work" from the average experience as produced, by the Holy Spirit, in faithful souls, was the only possible and correct one.

Now follows the substance of his observations on this point in the following synopsis: "Experience has moreover taught that, ordinarily, this state of Christian perfection is attained gradually by an upright course of life in following the Lamb; however, under this gradation, this work is perfected in the soul, sooner or later, by a sudden and powerful influence of grace and outpouring of the Divine Spirit. Those who have actually experienced it, describe this effusion of the Divine life as being similar to the grace of justification, yet far exceeding the same."

Ordinarily, then, there is a gradual attainment preceding the sudden completion of the work. There are exceptions to this rule, however, as the word "ordinarily" presupposes. The gradual attainment is characterized by "an *upright course* in following the Lamb," which is in contradistinction from a vascillating course of repeated backslidings and fresh starts. This upright course is not self-righteousness, it is subject to and governed by "following the Lamb." This following can be done only by faith, "for we *walk by faith*," and the upright course is the immediate fruit of faith in Christ. There is no time specified, nor even indicated, how long this gradual progress must last. The sentence, "This work is perfected in the soul, *sooner or later,*" perfectly ignores a fixed time. As all spiritual progress is governed by faith, and faith is governed by a close following of the light of the Holy Spirit and the Word of God, we may truly say that he who follows that light, and consequently his faith is increased proportionately, will come "*sooner*" to this glorious experience than he who hesitates to follow Divine leadings. The latter character will be just so much *"later"* as he makes it himself by not following the heavenly light. Faith is not bounded by time and space. As soon as we see in the light of God's Word and Spirit the need of salvation from all sin, we are invited to it without a moment's delay, for *"all things are now ready"* All things are possible to him that believeth, and all things are possible to the Holy Spirit. When faith and the Holy Spirit cooperate, the work is done. All postponement and aimless attitudes of soul are unscriptural and detrimental.

Another very important point has been settled by experience. There are a great many persons constitutionally unstable, many others not sufficiently watchful, a great many lack the necessary encouragement and help, and not a few meet with opposition instead of assistance. Considering besides these the many temptations and dangers surrounding the Christian, it is no wonder that this blessed state is sometimes lost, as our Article says: "Many others had attained it, but for want of watchfulness lost it again." What then? Shall we sit down in despair? Or shall we point at such unfortunate ones and say, "There! I expected nothing better! The work was not genuine—there is nothing in it," etc. By no means. By the grace of God *rise again!* For "experience has likewise taught that this blessed state, after it has been lost through negligence, may again be attained by the grace of God, and that a person may finally, after having been as a reed shaken by the wind, become as a firm and immovable pillar in the temple of God." Oh, the matchless grace of God, what wonders of mercy it can perform!

But let such a one now set a double watch at the dangerous point, and run the race for heaven with re- enforced energy. God can strengthen your weak constitutional points, and make you "steadfast and immovable, always abounding in the work of the Lord."

IV. Its Directions

And now we come to one of the most important points of the Article—its directions: "Let us, then, seriously and explicitly admonish all believers, ardently to strive for Christian Perfection." These words Mr. Wesley addressed to his preachers, and we have adopted them into our Discipline. Our preachers have all solemnly promised to "observe and defend the doctrines of faith and discipline of our Church," among which this doctrine stands preeminent. Their motto is to be "*Holiness to the Lord*" they are "to insist on inward and outward holiness," and "to build up the edifice of holiness on such a well laid foundation in every sermon."

How shall this be done? "Seriously and explicitly." Not in a superficial way, according to the letter, but "seriously," *from the heart*, as one who stands responsible to the Church and to God, who says, "Be be holy, for I am holy." Not in a general, aimless way, but "explicitly," pointing out clearly the *need*, the *want* and the present *possibility* of sanctification. And in order to accomplish the end of this preaching and of the passion and death of Christ (see Ephesians 5. 25, 26, 27), the Evangelical preacher is here directed to insist more particularly upon this "instantaneous work of grace," as described in this Article.

He is to urge the "gradual change zealously and continually," he is to preach up growth in grace, but the most effectual way to do this is "to insist upon an instantaneous change wrought, by the effusion of grace in an instant," for this good logical reason, "because the more earnestly this instantaneous work of grace is sought, the more it is longed for, the quicker and the more steadfastly the gradual work of grace in the soul will progress."

There is nothing more positively established in the range of experience and practice than that an aimless way of doing things will amount to nothing in the end. There must be an objective point that is to be reached, and if that point be attractive and attainable, the proper presentation of it to the mind will awaken desire, stir up energy, arouse activity; and progress toward it will be made as rapidly as possible. Hence "the more they are concerned about such a change, the more punctual they will be in observing the Divine ordinances… They are blessed in hope, and become so through this hope and expectation of a total change by gradually growing in grace."

On the other hand, when sanctification is preached in an indefinite manner, nothing will be accomplished: "Where this hope falls away, the work of grace begins to stagnate, if it does not apparently decrease; therefore, whosoever is concerned to promote the gradual growth in grace, should encourage believers in the hope of such an immediate influence of grace." A thousand times *Amen* to this proposition!

It is very evident that the Article does not in the least countenance metaphysical niceties or "hair-splittings" in preaching sanctification. Whether sin remains in believers in such a manner that it is only compressed, or depressed, by the influence of grace until sanctification removes it; whether a believer can be sanctified an hour after his conversion; whether he must make a new consecration, or simply keep intact that which he made in conversion; whether inbred sin is an entity or an inclination; whether sin is to be cast out first and then perfect love shed abroad, or whether the influence of perfect love casts out sin, etc., etc., is not said.

Our Article does not deal with these unpractical points. Neither is it necessary to know all about such matters, in order to become entirely sanctified. And it is, moreover, a question, whether something can ever be known about one or two of them, or whether they are not mere fancies. The Article is not made for a Nicodemus.

Sanctification is *practical*, and the Word and the Spirit

of God are the appointed guides of the seeker. Following them, he will be led into all truth, and that is sufficient.

Behold how much pride, avarice, envy, anger, peevishness under affliction, self-will, worldliness, and other "evil affections and desires" are still manifested in the Church! See the precious life-blood of the Son of God flowing to cleanse from all sin—until his Church become "holy, without spot, or wrinkle, or any such thing." Hear how God Jehovah commands, "Be ye holy, for I am holy!" Look how the world watches the Church to see the verification of her profession, "redeemed from all iniquity, and a peculiar people, zealous of good works!" Yea, how the principalities and powers of heaven gaze upon the Church to read in her experience of full salvation and holy life, as in a *living epistle,* the manifold wisdom of God, and the practical unfoldings of the "unsearchable riches of Christ!"

O brother minister! *You* are placed amidst these realities, called and appointed of God to bring the Church, as a chaste, pure virgin to her great Divine Bridegroom fitted for an eternal union. Oh, do for the sake of the Church, your Master and Saviour, and yourself, cease from "whittling fine points," and as in the sight of God and the judgment day fulfil your ordination vow, in that you *"seriously and explicitly admonish all believers ardently to strive for Christian Perfection."*

Further Statements and Directions

Again I turned my ear to the voice of the Discipline, to hear what the Church requires of the

Ministry,

and I heard these questions put to her candidates for preacher's license:

1. Have you obtained peace with God, in the pardon of your sins, through faith in Christ?

2. Have you the Spirit of God bearing witness with your spirit, that you are a child of God?

3. Is the love of God shed abroad in your heart by the Holy Spirit, in such a measure that you have complete victory over every sin, inwardly and outwardly? If not, do you earnestly desire it, do you seek it with all your heart?

Then I heard her give some General Rules and Directions for her preachers, and among other things she said: A preacher among us should be in such a state of grace, that no sin whatever have dominion over him, neither externally nor internally; and should this not be the case with him, he should strive without delay to become a partaker of perfect love; otherwise he cannot abide as a true Christian, much less as a teacher.

Let his motto be: *"Holiness unto the Lord"* To do the work of the Lord in the best manner the preacher must,

1. By exhortation and preaching, show the sinner the sinfulness of his condition, and convince him of the necessity of grace.

2. Point out Christ as the fountain of grace, and invite the sinner to accept of him through faith.

3. Build Up the edifice of holiness on such a well laid foundation; and do this in every sermon.

These things clearly convinced me that the Church demands a fully sanctified ministry—a ministry that lives in the experience of *"perfect love"* and that persistently seeks to lead all believers into the same experience.

A Prayer for Infant Sanctification

Again the voice of the Discipline falls upon my ear, and I hear a prayer for Infant Sanctification.

It is found in our ritual for Infant Baptism, and is a prayer, the import of which evidently is a supplication for *infant Sanctification*.

It reads thus:

"...O merciful God, thou who livest and reignest from everlasting to everlasting; thou didst give unto us thine only begotten Son, who shed out of his most precious side both water and blood, to cleanse us from sin, and gave commandment to his disciples that they should go and teach all nations, baptizing them in the name of the Father, and of the Son, and of the Holy Ghost; regard mercifully, we beseech thee, our supplication, and grant unto this child, now to be baptized, thy grace, as we bring it before thee by faith, in our prayers; wash, purify, sanctify and so prepare it by the Holy Spirit, that it may in future show itself an obedient child. Grant unto this child, O God, to become firm in faith, joyful in hope, and grounded in love; that the old Adam may be mortified and the new man be raised up; that all carnal and sinful propensities be rooted out, and new and spiritual desires take place and ever increase; that thus it may be enabled to conquer, and to reign over the devil, the flesh, and the world. O thou ever blessed God, vouchsafe to give unto this child the fulness of thy grace, that it may ever remain in the number of thy faithful and elect children... Amen."

The language of this prayer does not contemplate a condition of heart, in which there is sin *to be repented of*.

It could not do this consistently with either Scripture or reason. But it does contemplate a condition of heart in which *moral purity is not perfect*, but for the perfection, of which provision is made, in "the water and the blood shed out of the precious side" of the only begotten Son of God.

It assumes the presence both of "the old Adam" and of "the new man," and asks for the *destruction* of the former, and the *establishing* of the latter. It recognizes the indwelling of "carnal and sinful propensities," and implores God to *root them out* and put "new and spiritual desires" in their place, which shall "ever increase."

The advantage supposed to accrue to the child from the gifts here invoked, is that "it may be enabled to conquer, and to reign over the devil, the flesh and the world." This would seem to imply what is elsewhere in the Discipline defined as "*complete* victory over all sin, inwardly and outwardly," which is the fruit of "*perfect love.*"

But I quote again from the closing petition of this prayer, "O thou ever blessed God, vouchsafe to give unto this child the *fulness of thy grace*, that it may ever remain in the number of thy faithful and elect children." This sounds very much like a prayer for *full* salvation, and, as if remaining faithful, depended upon this "fulness."

I have not introduced this subject with a view of discussing the moral state of infants, but merely to show that the Church recognizes a possible moral condition *in which the human heart is neither under the dominion of sin, nor yet* FULLY *delivered from "carnal and sinful propensities."* Now, if such a condition does exist in the infant, may it not also be found in the adult who has been "converted and become as a little child"? Hence, the substance and spirit of the above prayer would be equally appropriate for "babes in Christ" (1 Cor. 3. 1.) or, for all who have not yet become "wholly sanctified." A prayer for the purification of those in whom the old Adam still exists, and, for the fulness of saving grace, is therefore in perfect accord with our Book of Discipline and, most emphatically so with the Bible. See John 17. 17 and 1 Thess. 5. 23.

That this thought is also contemplated by the Church, with reference to adult believers, is evident from the prayers connected with the formula for adult Baptism.

It must be assumed that the adult candidate for baptism is a believer—is converted. The first of these prayers includes petitions for "heavenly washing," for faith to "wholly overcome the world, the flesh, and Satan;" for the *raising* up of "the new man;" for the *mortification* of all "carnal affections," and for "the *fulness* of grace." Then follows this very significant prayer:

> "O merciful God, grant unto this person now to be baptized in thy name, the grace and the blessings of thy Holy Spirit, according to thy promise in Christ Jesus, thy well beloved Son, to give the Holy Spirit to all that ask thee. Thou who hast most graciously declared: 'Then will I sprinkle clean water upon you, and you shall be clean; from all your filthiness, and from all your idols will I cleanse you. And I will put my Spirit within you, and cause you to walk in my statutes, and you shall keep my judgments, and do them. O thou God of love, grant that this person may also be baptized with the Holy Spirit, and wholly dedicated to thee, and so endowed with strength Divine as to be able faithfully to perform his solemn promise made in the presence of this congregation, to wit: to have the victory over the devil, the world, and the flesh; to remain steadfast by a living faith in thy name, Father, Son and Holy Ghost; and at last, with the inmumerable company of thine elect, be triumphantly saved. Amen."

Now it is evident that "the grace and blessings" promised in the passage quoted in this prayer imply nothing less than *Entire* Sanctification. Hence, if this prayer be answered, the result will be the complete purification of the "person" or persons baptized. Thus the prayers connected with our Church ritual authorize us to pray for the sanctification of those who are in a state of justification before God. What else is the above form, but a prayer for *perfect* purity, and for the *full* baptism of the Holy Ghost?

"The Doctrines of the Evangelical Association"

In A.D. 1869, Bishop J. J. Esher, then Editor of the *Evangelical Magazine*, published his views in said monthly, especially on the doctrine of holiness, as held and formulated in *Our Catechism and Discipline*. The Catechism, from which he quotes, is the old one, compiled by Rev. W. W. Orwig. Since then, a new one has been compiled by the bishop himself, having been appointed thereto by the General Conference. Quotations from this new Catechism, will be found further on, showing that the author has not in the least changed his views respecting the distinct work of Entire Sanctification.

The following is a free translation from his Magazine editorial of 1869, on this subject:

> We hold our system of doctrine to be as complete, simple and clear, as any that can possibly be drawn from the Word of God by men, " Who have the Spirit of God." These doctrines have been divinely confirmed. — Here the Bishop quotes the following from the Catechism, in comparison with his own statements in a former editorial on the subject:
>
> What is meant by holiness or sanctification?
>
> By sanctification is meant the entire purification from all sin, and unreserved dedication to God, loving him with all our heart, with all our soul, with all our mind, and with all our strength; and our neighbor as ourselves.
>
> The proof-texts are 1 Thess. 5. 23; 1 Jno. 1. 7; and Matt. 22. 37-39.
>
> When does sanctification commence?
>
> Sanctification commences in regeneration, and must be continued to perfection. 1 Cor. 6. 11; Matt. 5. 48.

Here it is taught that the work of sanctification, through which we are entirely delivered from all that is sinful, and are perfected in the love of God, has its beginning in regeneration; hence, both regeneration and sanctification are the work of one Master, the Holy Spirit, and are one in essence and nature, but respecting the *fulness*, essentially different. Through sanctification, that is *completed* which was *begun* in regeneration; namely, the perfect moral restoration of man. As erroneous and unscriptural as it would be to speak of regeneration and sanctification as two entirely separate works, it is decidedly equally erroneous to speak of them as perfectly one and the same. The difference is not only in reference to gifts of the Spirit, but also in deliverance and purity from sin.

This is the view of our doctrine as contained in the Catechism, and it is certainly the holiness doctrine of the Word of God. The entire cleansing of the regenerated soul "from all sin, and unreserved dedication to God," is set forth as the main point in sanctification, from which we learn two essential points:

1. That the remaining "evil affections and desires" in the believer, are not in themselves harmless—they are "sin."

2. That the child of God is *entirely cleansed therefrom* in sanctification, and through this perfect cleansing and entire consecration to God, in love, the state of Christian perfection is reached. How thoroughly Biblical, how full of salvation, and how glorious is our doctrine!

Concerning the Article on Christian Perfection, as contained in the Discipline, the Bishop says:

> The whole Article, with all it contains, refers entirely and only to the believer, the child of God. Oh, that our entire membership were truly in possession of, and would carry out in their practice, the doctrine which the Church has so solemnly established in this Article!

In further commenting upon this important deliverance of the Church he says:

1. It is addressed to the believers, the converted, the children of God.

2. According to this doctrine they are afflicted with evil affections and desires as long as they are not entirely sanctified, and these evils are here called sin—essentially.

3. They can and must be fully redeemed from all sin long before they die.

4. This deliverance they can obtain instantaneous.

5. This points to the fact that faith is the condition of this deliverance.

6. Here we are taught that this work is *a change* which takes place in the believer, hence, sanctification is a distinct work from regeneration.

THE NEW CATECHISM

From this grand little book I quote the following questions and answers:—

Question 200. What is included in redemption?

Answer: Our deliverance from Satan, sin, and death, and our justification and sanctification as well as preservation, and eternal happiness through the death and triumph of Christ. Isa. 49. 25; Hosea 13. 14; Eph. 1. 7; 1 Cor. 1. 30.

Question 293. What is justification?

Justification is that act of God, whereby he forgives all our sins and recognizes us as righteous, through free grace, for the sake of Christ.—2 Cor. 5. 21; Eph. 1. 7; Rom. 4. 7, 8.

Question 295. What is regeneration, which takes place at the same time with justification?

Regeneration is a work of the triune God, which God the Holy Spirit accomplishes in us, in that he awakens us from the death of sin, and makes us partakers of the Divine nature, and the Divine life.— John 3. 16; 1

Pet. 1. 3; John 1. 12; John 3. 14, 15; John 3. 7; Tit. 3. 5-7; Eph. 2. 5, 6; Rom. 5. 5.

Question 301. What is Sanctification?

Sanctification is that work of the Holy Spirit in us, whereby we are wholly sanctified, or, as the Apostle Paul expresses it: sanctified through and through.

(This latter phrase is a literal translation from the German, of 1 Thess. 5. 23. H. J. B.)—2 Thess. 2. 13; 1 Pet. 1. 2; 1 Thess. 5. 23.

Question 302. Wherein consisteth Entire Sanctification?

Entire Sanctification consists in purification from all sin or the destruction of all evil affections and desires, and in our entire renewal and perfect consecration of spirit, soul and body to the service and praise of God.—2 Cor. 7. 1; 1 John 1. 7, 9; Col. 3. 9, 10; Rom. 6. 11.

Question 303. What is the divine condition of our Sanctification?

The divine condition of our Sanctification is faith in Jesus Christ.—Acts 15. 9; Acts 26. 18.

Question 304. How does this faith of the child of God prove itself?

By our walking in the light, denying ourselves of all ungodliness and worldly lusts, childlike fidelity toward God, and resignation to his will, a heartfelt desire for the fulness of salvation in Christ, and a confident appropriation of the same to ourselves.—1 John 1. 7; Tit. 2. 12; Rom. 12. 1; Matt. 5. 6.

Question 305. "What are the means through which the Holy Spirit effects the work of Sanctification in the children of God?

The word of God, and the blood of Jesus Christ, the Son of God.—John 17. 17; Heb. 9. 14; Rev. 1. 5.

Question 306. What does Sanctification effect?

Christian Perfection.—Matt. 5. 48.

Question 307. Wherein consisteth Christian Perfection?

In being pure, and being minded as Jesus our pattern was, and walking even as he walked.—1 John 3. 3; Phil. 2. 5; 1 John 2. 6; John 4. 34; John 8. 29.

Question 308. Whereby does Christian Perfection prove itself?

Herein, that we in truth love God perfectly, and our neighbor as ourselves, and thus keep the commandments of God.— Matt. 22. 37-40; John 14. 23; 1 John 4. 12; 1 John 5. 2, 3; Matt. 5. 44.

Question 309. What is the effect of Christian Perfection?

A constant increase or growth in divine knowledge and spiritual strength, as well as fruitfulness in good works, to the glory of God, and in the blessedness of this state of grace.—2 Pet. 3. 18; Col. 1. 9-12.

Question 310. Who obtains this state of Sanctification and Christian Perfection?

It is the calling and privilege of every Christian to be sanctified through and through, already in this life, and to be without blame before God in love, and thus walk in the commandments of God.—1 Thess. 4. 3, 4, 7; 1 Pet. 1. 15, 16; Eph. 1. 4; Luke 1. 6.

Such is the language of the book specially prepared for the purpose of indoctrinating the youth of our Church in her distinctive views and doctrines.

OUR HYMN-BOOK THEOLOGY ON HOLINESS

In her voice of song the Evangelical Association is no less definite and pronounced in favor of experimental holiness than in her Discipline and her Catechism.

Her new Hymn-Book contains no less than *thirty-one* hymns on "Entire Sanctification," some of which express very definitely, the prayer of a soul seeking full salvation, and expecting it *now*.

What else are we taught in hymn number 376, under the inscription, "Prayer For the Refining Fire"?

Who but a truly converted soul can sing the first line? And who but one expecting perfect purity *just now* can sing these verses "with the spirit and with the understanding:"

> My God, I know, I feel thee mine,
>   And will not quit my claim,
> Till all I have is lost in thine,
>   And all renewed I am.
>
> 2 I hold thee with a trembling hand,
>   And will not let thee go,
> Till steadfastly by faith I stand,
>   And all thy goodness know.
>
> 3 Jesus, thine all-victorious love
>   Shed in my heart abroad:
> Then shall my feet no longer rove,
>   Rooted and fixed in God.
>
> 4 Oh, that in me the sacred fire
>   Might now begin to glow!
> Burn up the dross of base desire,
>   And make the mountains flow!
>
> 5 Oh, that it now from heaven might fall,
>   And all my sin consume!
> Come, Holy Ghost, for thee I call,
>   Spirit of burning, come.
>
> 6 Refining fire, go through my heart,
>   Illuminate my soul;
> Scatter thy life through every part,
>   And sanctify the whole.

Or number 378, from which we sing:

> O Jesus, at thy feet we wait,
>   Till thou shalt bid us rise,
> Restored to our unsinning state,
>   To love's sweet Paradise.
> 2 Since thou wouldst have us free from sin,
>   And pure as those above,
> Make haste to bring thy nature in,
>   And perfect us in love.

Then we turn to number 389, and our desires and prayers grow more intense as we sing:

> Dear Jesus, I long to be perfectly whole;
> I want thee forever to live in my soul;
> Break down every idol, cast out every foe:
> Now wash me, and I shall be whiter than snow.
>
> Cho.—Whiter than snow, yes, whiter than snow;
> Now wash me, and I shall be whiter than snow.
>
> 2 Dear Jesus, come down from thy throne in the skies,
> And help me to make a complete sacrifice;
> I give up myself, and whatever I know—
> Now wash me, and I shall be whiter than snow.
>
> 3 Dear Jesus, for this I most humbly entreat;
> I wait, blessed Lord, at thy crucified feet,
> By faith for my cleansing, I see thy blood flow—
> Now wash me, and I shall be whiter than snow.

Here our prayer and faith are supposed to reach their climax, and our joyous song breaks out in praise and profession, as we sing:

The blessing by faith, I receive from above;
Oh, glory! my soul is made perfect in love;
My prayer has prevailed, and this moment I know,
The blood is applied, I am whiter than snow.

These are only a few specimens of our prayers *for* and profession *of* entire sanctification, as we sing them from our Church Hymn-Book; in our social worship, and in our public congregations. Would that the holiness theology of our hymns would become a burning, blazing reality, in the heart of every one whose voice chimes in with our sweet and sacred melodies.

On the *use* of hymns a recent writer makes the following pertinent remarks:

"A hymn either means what it says, or it does not. If it means a certain thing, let it be used as an expression of that thing, or not used at all. There is no difference between singing a truth, and saying that truth in the ordinary tones of the speaking voice. A spoken untruth is not divested of its inherent falsehood when it is set to music and sung, however artistically. We have no right to say to the Lord God: 'Here's my heart, oh, take and seal it,' unless we mean just that. If we sing, 'Thus far the Lord hath led me on,' it should be with a reverent and deep sense of the Divine guidance of our lives, from youth to the present day-. We insult the Master if we exclaim,

'Jesus, I my cross have taken,
All to leave and follow thee,'—

if we have never taken up our cross at all, or, having done so, have no idea of leaving anything in particular, or of following Christ in any direction opposite to our own desires. The prayer—

'Rock of Ages, cleft for me,
Let me hide myself in thee' —

is a prayer, not a vain repetition.
"When a hymn is read, it should be followed with attention to the close; when it is sung, it should be made, so far as possible, a part of one's own spiritual exercises, aspirations, or resolutions. If you do not believe the words of a hymn, or cannot utilize them, — and hymns are not always perfect or scriptural, — do not sing them. But if you *do* believe them, sing them as a real expression of your belief, or, at any rate, listen to them in the same spirit with which you listen to the minister when he prays or preaches."

This is sound reasoning. We certainly must not think lightly of our theology as expressed in song. We might as well treat it indifferently in any other of its forms of expression.

Having heard these formulated views and doctrines of the Church, in statements, directions, resolutions and song, and also the comments upon them from recognized leaders among us, I turn in the direction of the founders and fathers of our Church. — Here the first voice that salutes my eager ear is from

Albright, Walter and Miller

A record left by Rev. George Miller, of Mr. Albright, from which I gather the unmistakable fact that Albright both enjoyed the grace of entire sanctification himself and was greatly concerned about having others enjoy it.

His motto was "Holiness unto the Lord." Christian Perfection was his aim, of which he had a deep, Scriptural, Methodistic conception. He strove earnestly for this state of grace and obtained and enjoyed it, according to his own testimony, and that of others who knew him. Entire Sanctification was with him by no means a "glittering generality," but a Scriptural truth and a blessed reality. "He enjoyed and practiced perfect love toward God and man, and was, through the grace of God, completely master of his affections and desires, and subjected them all to the rule of the Spirit." Such is the testimony given concerning him, by one who knew him quite well. He held this doctrine to be all-important, and impressed it by preaching, and otherwise, very frequently upon preachers and members. — Having met Mr. Miller one day, in great heaviness, he spoke words of comfort and courage to him and asked him "whether he had obtained the grace of perfect Sanctification." To this Miller replied, "I cannot say that I have."

"Then," continued Mr. Albright, "you cannot preach, holiness with power," and exhorted Miller to seek this grace earnestly and without delay; otherwise he could not endure severe trials. "For," said he, "the devil will often attack you; therefore seek this grace in order to withstand him, and that you may accept all crosses and adversities willingly and thankfully, as from the hand of the Lord."

Mr. Miller says: "This sank deep into my heart, and *with tears I asked God to sanctify my soul*. And, several times such a gracious power came upon me, that I could heartily thank God for all sufferings. Still the certainty of this state of grace in me was disturbed for awhile, because I did not fully comprehend the deep depravity of human nature. I desired to be perfectly delivered from all evil affections and desires; wherefore, I once spent nearly a whole day in prayer and supplication. Thus the Lord brought me nearer and nearer to Entire Sanctification, so that I could more and more confidently trust that God would bless me and give me the unction of the Holy Ghost, that I might be able to triumph over Satan, the world and sin." On another occasion these two brethren spent a few days in company with each other, when Mr. Miller again complained of his trials, to which Albright replied: "This is indeed a heavy burden, but it is our own fault that you are so overwhelmed, for you are not willing to submit to the hand of God, and as long as this is the case the Lord will not change your condition. But of this be certain, that if you were perfectly saved from these infirmities, and would stand fast in this salvation, you would not only cease complaining of your sufferings, and be resigned to the leadings of the Lord; but you would even praise and thank God, for everything that may befall you." Miller says: "With such words he urged me to submit entirely to God, to be content with my condition, and earnestly follow after holiness.

> "This admonition so affected my heart, that during a journey of about thirty miles I wept nearly all the way; and in the evening I wrestled about one hour in prayer, until a powerful stream of love poured down upon me, so that I could love and praise God for all my crosses and sufferings. Yea, I could love my bitterest enemies, and persecutors, and thank God for the manifold chastenings that had come upon me. I knew certainly that all things must work together for my good, and I felt willing to 'kiss the rod.' Glory, praise and honor, to my Father and my God! O that I could praise Thee forever! From this time on I could preach and speak with much more clearness on the subject of holiness; but I did not trust to profess it as my experience, until I was tested at several 'big meetings' and at one Conference. But the Lord helped me mightily in this."

At a later date, when Mr. Miller had completed his compilation of the Book of Discipline, he says: "I was exceedingly anxious that I should first be found obeying these things which I had written for others. But God would have me tested; for, at an annual conference session, I had to testify concerning Entire Sanctification, which I believed I had experienced, and, also to my professed obedience, to our Book of Discipline. But I was enabled to give testimony to these things to the great comfort and improvement of my soul, and the satisfaction of my brethren. I thank God from the depths of my heart that he assured me more than ever on this occasion of the irresistible influx of his love,"...

"From this time on I realized the grace of Sanctification in such a measure, and such quickening power, that in preaching *I had to profess it publicly in order to satisfy my convictions*; for the doctrine of holiness flowed involuntarily from my lips, so that I could say with certainty before God and the Church, *'It is not I, but the grace of God in me.'* This doctrine of holiness was blessed of the Lord *to the good of many of my brethren, and caused me great joy.* And, some of them attained to such confidence, that by the next annual conference they had outstripped me. Blessed be the name of our gracious and merciful God, who has thus-blessed and spread the doctrine of holiness to the good of so many!"

Unfaithful Ministers Cannot be Sanctified

Mr. Miller says, "when a preacher fails to follow his calling the work of grace in him will soon begin to stagnate. In the first place he cannot teach holiness correctly and savingly; and in the next place he cannot judge of the doctrine properly when he hears others preach it, and thirdly, he cannot help his erring brethren into the right way. If he attempts it he will only cause the more damage. I am fully convinced of this by observation, having heard a preacher teach holiness erroneously, and not as I experienced it and learned from the Holy Scriptures to teach holiness.

The Grace of Sanctification Defined

"The grace of Sanctification is perfect victory in us, through Christ, so that all temptations to sin are instantly repelled and overcome. Hence, that which is evil, or sinful has no power over the sanctified, either inwardly or outwardly. But such persons must by no means conclude that there is no more danger of being tempted to sin. There is great reason why they should watch, and work out their salvation with fear and trembling. Yet, be assured that the grace of God, in Christ Jesus, is stronger than Satan, the world or the flesh. Whoever does not voluntarily let this grace slip, but continues therein by watching and prayer unto the end, will be kept from all sin and preserved unto eternal life.

"With this grace I was enabled to deal with all persons, rich or poor, relative or stranger, without respect of persons, and this also greatly aided me in setting forth true Practical Christianity." This last statement refers to a book written by Mr. Miller, entitled "Practical Christianity," from which I quote the following plain statement of his views:—

> Holiness, or Christian Perfection, which Christ requires of his disciples and all true believers, (Matt. 5. 48.), he will also cheerfully grant unto all who desire it with their whole heart, and seek it by believing and confident prayer in true humility and submission, surrendering all self-will, and humbling himself under the hand of God. Whosoever will surrender himself, soul and body, unto God, and by faith lay hold upon the sanctifying love of Christ, will soon attain to the happy state of grace in which he submits to all the sufferings and afflictions of this life as coming from the hand of God, not only with resignation, but also with gratitude. Hence he can love God with all his heart, soul and strength; reign over all his spiritual enemies, and successfully resist every temptation the moment it is presented, without yielding, as is often the case with weak Christians. In this happy state of grace the Christian stands firm and immovable by watching and prayer,

and his joy and peace resting in God, are not easily interrupted. This is called *sanctification,* and in order to retain it we must constantly live near to God, Oh! what a glorious privilege the sanctified person enjoys, being rooted and grounded in God, and surrounded by his love like a wall of fire; God dwells in him, and he in God. Against such a soul sin has as it were lost all its power; for he is enclosed in the fear of the Lord, protected by his power, continually obtaining comfort and peace from God under all afflictions and trials — but not without watching and prayer. According to the admonition of the apostle, such a soul can rejoice ever more, pray without ceasing, and in everything give thanks, for such is the will of God in Christ Jesus.

Dear reader, from the passages of Scripture quoted, it appears very evident that it is essentially necessary to strive after holiness, and hold fast the same when once obtained. Whosoever neglects this does not obey the will of God, but follows his own will, and that of the world, and of Satan. Therefore let every one take heed not to neglect and despise the grace of God. And he that has neglected to seek sanctifying grace, or having once enjoyed it, but through carelessness lost it, such I would exhort in the spirit of the apostle, raise the feeble hands, strengthen the weak knees, and make straight paths for your feet, lest that which is lame be turned out of the way, but let it rather be healed. (Heb. 12. 12, 13.) Give yourself up to the will of God entirely, fully surrendering all self, as I have shown, and continue in earnest, believing prayer, and God, the giver of all good and perfect gifts, will not delay to impart the Holy Spirit to your sanctification. Should it even seem as though the Lord would not bestow such grace, only continue steadfast in watching and prayer until help comes; for "they that wait upon the Lord shall renew their strength; they shall mount up with wings as eagles; they shall run and not be weary, and they shall walk and not faint." (Isa. 40. 31.)

He that has obtained this grace from God, so as to be a continual conqueror and constant victor, must, nevertheless, still continue to grow in divine knowledge and love, in connection with steady watching and prayer. Negligence in progressing from glory to glory in the knowledge of God, is as irreconcilable with sanctifying grace, as it is impossible to retain the state of justification without advancing to sanctification by watching and prayer. The sanctified Christian can and must continually abound more and more in this state of grace, must make advancement, as much as lieth in his power, not by slow degrees, but if he is truly in earnest, really desirous to continue steadfast in the grace of God, he will, like Paul, press forward toward the mark of the prize of our high calling of God in Christ Jesus. (Phil. 3. 5.) This is the sense in which the apostle speaks in the 13th verse: "Brethren, I count not myself to have apprehended; but this one thing I do, forgetting those things which are behind, and reaching forth unto those things which are before." The apostle's idea at this place is not that he himself has not obtained holiness or a clean heart, as some erroneously claim. Far from it. He speaks of the *heavenly* prize, of the crown of life, for which he was striving, and wished to encourage his brethren in this respect to follow his example. I am assured that whosoever will fight the good fight of faith after the manner of the primitive Christians, continue in watching and prayer, and go forward from one degree of grace to another, he can also remain steadfast until it shall please God at last to relieve him from the infirmities of this tabernacle of flesh. This state of grace; this new and spiritual life with Christ in God; such progress in life unto sanctification and perfection in Christianity; such steady progress from one glory to another, such firmness in God with constant watching and prayer; in short, this happy state, attainable already in this life, is the most contented, happy and prosperous state that one could wish to be in. Therefore let us give heed to the exhortation of the apostle: "Wherefore the rather, brethren, give diligence to make your calling and election sure; for if you do these things, ye shall never fall." (2 Pet. 1. 10.)

Rev. John Walter

It is to be regretted that so few of the words of this golden tongued orator have been left on record; of whom Rev. Dr. Schmucker, of the Lutheran Church, once said, "He is profoundly learned, and a speaker that has scarcely yet been excelled." His learning, however, consisted in a knowledge of the things of God, which enabled him, as a true "son of thunder" to astonish the people with his powerful speech.

The following sermon will give the reader some idea of his views on holiness, and his style of preaching. It was preached in the open air in 1802, and reported years afterward, from memory, by Father Wonder, of Cary, Ohio.

> Text—Who is she that looketh forth as the morning, fair as the moon, clear as the sun, and terrible as an army with banners?—Sol. Songs 6. 10.
>
> Beloved Hearers: Come and consider with me these glorious words of the wise man, Solomon. In his Songs he speaks of Christ the heavenly Bridegroom, and of true Christians as his Bride. In our text he represents Christ as expressing his love, joy and admiration for his bride. Behold, what love this language indicates, and then look to Calvary, where it was exhibited in a manner unheard of before. Here Jesus offered up his life for the purchase of his Bride, and our text gives a beautiful description of how he gradually prepared her for himself. Each person belonging to this bride knows

something of this by experience.

I. "*Who is she that looketh forth as the morning?*" The morning pre-supposes darkness. The sinner belongs to the kingdom of darkness. He lives in darkness, performs the works of darkness—is darkened in his understanding, heart and will. Such are called the "children of night." Their condition answers to that of the earth when it was "without form and void," and when "darkness was upon the face of the deep." But Jesus, who is the "Light of the world," arises as the Sun of Righteousness unto such souls, and their first light in the heart is as the breaking forth of the morning light. But to such souls the day has not yet fully come. Yet, at this dawning they see, partially, their sins, and the misery of their condition.

In this condition the sinner appears, in the sight of heaven, earth and hell, as the promising morning dawn—such "go forth" and draw attention to themselves. The world, which loveth darkness rather than light, will persecute them. Now when they begin to forsake the works of darkness wicked men will accuse them of the sins they committed, together; Satan also, will seek to hinder them, but Jesus and holy angels rejoice greatly over them, as they break forth from their darkness into the kingdom of light, the certainty of their pardon, and the witness of their adoption.

II. "*Fair as the moon,*" such souls now shine in their lives. Not in their own light, or righteousness, but like the moon reflecting the light of the sun; so do they reflect the light of Christ. They are now the children of the day—*a light in the Lord.* There is light in their understanding and in their hearts, and they know that they are on the way of life. Still, with them this light diminishes and increases as it does with the moon. In all spiritual understanding they are only children. Sometimes, in hours of trial their light is as dim as the new moon, and generally they live only in the light of the quarter-moon where they learn to know many besetments and remains of sin, in their feelings, words and works. The seasons when they represent the beautiful full moon are usually short. They have remission of sins, and, like the moon, are almost constantly floating in the light of the sun. The changes in their feelings, etc., are not permanent, and if they will only continue to walk in the light as God is in the light they will soon be,

III. "*Clear as the sun*" in the enjoyment of entire sanctification, since, by faith, Christ dwells in their hearts, and his light shines forth from their entire being, in holiness and true righteousness. Such Christians are then fully separated from the world—chosen and precious in the sight of God, through Jesus Christ. They are cleansed from all unrighteousness, love God with all their heart and their neighbor as themselves. Such persons are under the command and leadership of the Prince of our Salvation.

IV. "*Terrible as an army with banners.*" There is a severe conflict between Christ and Satan—between righteousness and sin. Christ must reign till he hath put all his enemies under his feet. All true Christians belong to his army, and are led by this great Prince of glory. This army consists of various divisions with their banners, but as they are all "Saints of the Most High," they are united, and present a terrible front to the legions of hell. It is said that

"Satan trembles when he sees,
 The *weakest saint* upon his knees."

In the name of Jesus they conquer. Sinners will be rescued from the jaws of Satan. Throughout entire communities, families and hearts, his works are laid in ruins, for, "For this purpose the Son of God was manifested, that he might destroy the works of the devil." Thus the Christians go forth, with Christ as their Captain, conquering their enemies upon the right hand and the left. Hear it, ye people, and take it to heart: The true Christian people, if faithful to their exalted Leader, will take this country, and finally they will appear with Christ and his heavenly host when he shall come in power, with ten thousands of angelic attendants, and with flaming fire, to take vengeance on them that know not God, and are not obedient to the Gospel of our Lord Jesus Christ, banishing them from the presence of God, and from the glory of his power, to writhe in eternal pain. This appearing of Christ will be glorious, with all his saints who believed on him, and obediently followed him. Then all the ungodly, and the scorners, shall be like straw for the devouring flames, while the children of God shall appear with him in glory. Then, while ten thousand thunders will be rolling, and the heavens be blazing with forked tongues of lightning; while the plowshare of ruin shall run deep through world on world, and a universal fire shall lick up the waters of the great oceans, then shall the wicked cry, "Ye rocks and mountains, fall on us and cover us from the face of him that sitteth on the throne, and from the wrath of the Lamb, for the great day of his wrath is come and who shall be able to stand?" Then shall the saints shine in the glory of the Son of God, while they shall help to judge the world.

Sinner, hear it! The Son of God, whom you are crucifying, and whose blood you trampled beneath your unholy feet, and the praying followers of Jesus will, in the last day, meet you in their glory, but "terrible as an army with banners," to drive you into the lake that burneth with fire and brimstone! Before this terrible army you will retreat as before a storm of thunder bolts from heaven, to take up your abode where there is wailing and gnashing of teeth. In that day "every eye shall see him, and they also, which pierced him, and all kindreds of the earth shall *wail because of him.*"

Then shall all the children of God rejoice greatly, and the saints of the Most High shall take possession of the kingdom forever and ever. "Songs and everlasting joy shall be upon their heads; they shall obtain joy and gladness, and sorrow and sighing shall flee away."

Hallelujah! Amen.

But *hark*! I hear another voice, which has in it the clear ring of the old Holiness Trumpet, and as I turn to see whence it comes, I read the name of

REV. JOHN DREISBACH

Bro. John Dreisbach was the first Presiding Elder of the Evangelical Association. From a record written by his own hand concerning a camp-meeting held at Conewago, Pa., in June, 1814, I quote the following:

> "June 1. To-day the friends assembled, and in the evening Bro. Schauer preached and H. Niebel exhorted.
>
> "I felt a great concern for the meeting, and had faith for the conversion of sinners and the sanctification of believers.
>
> "June 2. To-day I preached from 1 Pet. 1 22, 'Seeing ye have purified your souls in obeying the truth through the Spirit unto unfeigned love of the brethren, see that ye love one another with a pure heart fervently.' Great grace was upon me, and I felt a wonderful solemnity for sinners. Several fell down as though they were dead. The friends were deeply convinced of the necessity of Sanctification. At 2 o'clock P. M., Bro. Erb preached on the trembling of Felix under Paul's preaching, after which I exhorted the penitents *now* to look to Jesus by faith, and told the friends, they should

believe unto sanctification, *and called upon all who were willing to do this to hold up their hands*. They did so, and we began to pray. There was a special purifying power from God among us. Many, according to their profession, obtained sanctifying power. I do not know that I ever felt the power of God stronger in me than to-day, while I was preaching on holiness. My body and soul were refreshed, *and I felt, myself what I preached unto others. Blessed be God for this*!

This meeting was richly blessed with conversions and experiences of holiness."

Of another Camp-Meeting held the same year, he says: "The preaching of the Law and the Gospel worked mightily unto sanctification." And again he says, "To my knowledge, I never heard sounder confessions of holiness than I heard here, while many others deeply felt the need of it."

A year later he says: "God gave me abundant grace to preach justification and sanctification through faith. The power unto conversion and sanctification came upon us. Thank God, it penetrated body and soul!

> "I believe many of the friends were renewed and established in holiness. The result of this meeting was, that fourteen were converted and *twenty-eight* professed holiness."

Still later he reports a meeting at which "twenty- four were converted, and sixteen professed holiness." Thus we see the earnestness, and some of the methods, by which this gifted man of blessed memory sought to promote the experience of entire sanctification among believers, or converted souls, whom he designates as "the friends." Nor did he ever change his views of the importance of this matter, as may be seen from a letter written to the author of his biography (Rev. R. Yeakel) in 1869, just a year or two before his death. "In this letter," says his Biographer, "he expressed his great joy over the so-called 'Holiness movement,' through which has been brought about an earnest seeking and wrestling to apprehend Christ fully, as he is made of God, unto our Sanctification."

His letter closes with the following words of solicitude for the doctrine of holiness as hitherto accepted and taught among us:

> "The doctrine of Christian Perfection, which from the beginning was contained in our Book of Discipline, was considered by the fathers as the *established* doctrine of the Evangelical Association, on Christian Holiness, and I hope our Church will always hold fast, and faithfully teach and live this *truly Scriptural doctrine.* Should, however, a time come when the Evangelical Association would cast away and disregard this doctrine, then 'Ichabod' should be written in its stead, because then the glory of Israel would be departed. Let us hope and pray that this may never come to pass, but that our Israel may go up and possess the land, and God be glorified forever."

But I turn my ear to another voice from the sainted fathers, and this time I hear a clear, strong blast from the silver trumpet of

Rev. Henry Fisher

"Full of faith and the Holy Ghost," his ministry extended over a period of *twenty-three* years—1831-1854—during which time he served as pastor, or rather traveling preacher, Presiding Elder, General Book Agent, and Editor of the *Evangelical Messenger*, in succession.

I have before me a brief sketch of one of. his sermons, from the text, "Blessed are the pure in heart, for they shall see God."

He begins by saying: "I do not come to you with critical definitions and descriptions of those who are pure in heart, but will simply repeat the Biblical representations of their character. They are those who love God with all their heart, soul, mind, and strength, and their neighbor as themselves. They are crucified with Christ and can say with Paul, 'I live, yet not I but *Christ liveth in me.*' They reckon themselves dead, indeed, unto sin and alive unto God, through Christ Jesus our Lord. They *have washed* their robes and made them white in the blood of the Lamb. They are continually a living sacrifice unto God that is holy and acceptable, which is their reasonable service. They have their conversation in heaven—forgetting the things that are behind, they press forward for the crown of life, and meanwhile shine as a light in the world, and in themselves they enjoy, through Christ, that perfect love which casteth out all fear that hath torment, and gives them boldness to stand in the day of Judgment. And, though they are still on probation, and must fight, and suffer with Christ, yet they come off more than conquerors through Him that loved them. Blessed state!

> "They are *blessed* because they *are pure*. The impurities of sin are taken away—the sinful affections and desires destroyed, and the sanctified powers of the soul acting in harmony according to God's will."

"Holiness Our Chief Topic"

During Mr. Fisher's editorship he wrote for the *Evangelical Messenger* of 1849, as follows:

> "The doctrine of holiness, or entire sanctification, *ought to be at all times our chief topic*, because it is the top, as well as the cornerstone of Christianity. It is the substance of Christian experience, and *the heart of the religion of Jesus Christ*. Take away the doctrine of full re-

demption, and its being ready and offered *to-day* and *now* (2 Cor. 6. 2.), and the salt will have lost its savor, and God's dear children will be destitute of that food which their heavenly Father has provided for them in the Gospel. And, if the Gospel of Christ be 'the power of God unto salvation to every one that "believeth' (Rom. 1. 16.), if 'all things are *now* ready' (Luke 14. 17.), and if the end of our preaching shall be, 'that we present every man perfect in Christ Jesus (Col. 1. 28.), *then every minister of the Gospel should try to hold forth this doctrine in its purity (and, unless this is done, the Church under our charge will sink), and every believer ought to use his utmost endeavors to come up to the very standard of Christian perfection.* Moreover, *as this is the doctrine of our Church, of the Church of Christ, and of the Bible, we should be firm and immovable, recommending it by example and precept wherever we are, and, trusting in the Lord, stand as men of courage in its defence.*"

These are plain words from one who stood second to none of our now sainted teachers as to his saintly life, his Church loyalty, etc. The importance he here attaches to the experience of entire sanctification is put in as specific and strong language as any modern holiness editor or preacher could well employ. How different from many preachers of our day!

It is a serious fact, that this very work, which ought to be our chief topic, is persistently suppressed by some who have vowed to promote it—to "exhort all believers to become partakers of perfect love," *Brother*, pay thy vows.

Holiness must be Sought

The following is from the German of Rev. H. Fisher. The word holiness is a very comprehensive term and should by all means be correctly understood by every person, especially by every professor of religion.

God spake already to his ancient people, saying, "Ye shall be holy; for I am holy." Lev. 11. 44. Peter, when exhorting and encouraging believers to self-denial, growth in grace and zeal, says: "Not fashioning yourselves according to the former lusts in your ignorance; but as he which hath called you, is holy, so be ye holy in all manner of conversation; ("All manner of *living*.— Revised Version) because it is written, Be he holy, for I am holy." 1 Pet. 1. 14-16. Many more passages might be quoted to establish this ground, but these will suffice.

From these passages and from the Scriptures generally, it is evident that God wants us to be holy—to seek and enjoy holiness.

By the term holiness we understand entire freedom and separation from all sin, perfect cleansing from all filthiness of the flesh and spirit, and to be transformed into such a state that we are enabled to love God with all the heart, with all the soul, with all the mind, with all our strength, and our neighbor as ourselves; and can say: "For this is the love of God, that we keep his commandments, and his commandments are not grievous." 1 John 5. 3.

But we do not wish to be understood to believe that the Christian can attain to such a degree of holiness in this world as to be free from all ignorance, and all imperfections, pertaining to his understanding, his mental capacities, and his judgment—that he will have no more temptations—no more trials and crosses to bear— or that he will discover no more infirmities in himself, nor be in danger of falling from grace and losing his soul. But we believe and declare, on the authority of God's word, and the experience of *many*, that he can be so crucified to the world, and the world to him— and that he can be so filled with the love of God that he is able, under all circumstances, to lead a holy life, and to serve the Lord with joy and thanks-giving. 1 Thess. 5. 16-18, 23, 24. We further declare that when the believer has reached this state, he can still become more closely united with God, through Christ, and that the only way to retain this grace is, to be continually going forward.

Again he writes thus: Destitute of the sanctifying power, we are not moving in the sphere in which God would have us, and as a natural consequence, *are not able* to perform the work assigned to, or the duties incumbent on us, so as to meet the approbation of the great Head of the Church. Whether you are a minister, an official, or a private member—a husband or wife— parent or child—master, mistress, or servant—let your relation in life be what it may, *you are dependent on sanctifying grace* to discharge the various duties enjoined upon you; and without holiness of heart *it is impossible* for any one to serve God in accordance with his holy and righteous will, and consequently whosoever neglects to strive after it, violates the precepts of the Most High. The command in relation to this work is as plain, and as binding on us as any one in the Bible; and, therefore, he who does not comply with the requirements of the Gospel, will, sooner or later, yield to the temptations of the devil—nature will be revived, and he will fall a victim to the enemies of his immortal soul. We need not wonder that there are so many worldly-minded and cold-hearted professors, who are clogging the Church, and are a hindrance to the promotion of religion, and that there are so many backsliders in the world, who, wallowing, as it were, in the mire of unrighteousness, are of the most miserable creatures on the surface of the earth—when we consider that there is, generally, so little exertion made, and the momentous duty of striving for entire sanctification is so rarely insisted upon.

The blessedness which he enjoys who commits himself *entirely to the Lord*, and the love imparted to him from our Heavenly Father, cannot be discovered to such as are unacquainted with the nature of religion. It must be experienced.

Considering these things, should not every one be induced, with all earnestness, to strive for holiness of heart and life? How are you minded? What are your sentiments in regard to this important work? *Are you enjoying the blessing of entire sanctification? If not, are you striving for it?* or are you at ease in Zion? If so, may God alarm you! Do commence the work *now* — do not rest satisfied with a mere form of godliness, or with what you once experienced; but give your whole heart to Jesus, and strive for a bright witness of your adoption; and if you feel yourself in a state of Justification, go ahead — search the Scriptures *and read such publications as will convey light on the subject*. Meditate — breathe the spirit of prayer — agonize and watch in prayer — search your heart — be zealous of good works; and at all times exercise faith in the all-sufficiency of the blood of Christ. In all your exercises look to Jesus, and expect *the blessing as a free gift of God*, and be willing to receive it in his own way; and you may take it for granted that the Holy Spirit will accomplish the work as soon as you are altogether willing to commit yourself to the Lord, and lay all upon the altar.

At another time he wrote: It is absolutely necessary that every professor of religion strive to become a partaker of this grace. The fact that it is God's will (1 Thess. 4. 3.; Heb. 12. 14.) is a sufficient reason why every one should consider it his duty to seek and retain this state of grace. Even though a person be justified from his sins, unless he follows after holiness, he is disobedient, and will fail in the end. His own nature, the world, and Satan, will be too strong for him, and he will be carried away with the current of unrighteousness. This is the principal reason why so many who had once obtained the grace of God are now in perdition,—why many who once flourished in the Church of Christ, are again running with the world, and revelling in unrighteousness—and others, although they are still carried along as members, are, as it were, swallowed up in frivolity, love of the world, and pride; so that they are only a burden to the Church, and unless they again are thoroughly *converted*, they will be lost with all their profession. May the dear Lord, for Jesus' sake, pour out his Spirit largely upon the entire Christian world, so that the Church may wake up to this important and divinely ordered cause.

> If sinners are to be truly converted through the instrumentality of the Church, her members must be sanctified. But the question arises, how is this grace obtained? We answer, by being sincere in all things, as far as we have knowledge, exercising ourselves in self-denial, being zealous unto all good works, yet not trusting in our own works, but looking unto Jesus, by faith, and believing that there is full power in the atonement of Christ to redeem us from all uncleanness, and to transform us into a state of holiness. We must exercise faith, and, since grace is obtained through faith, we have a right, when we sincerely and earnestly discharge all our duties, to expect it at this time, yes, even now. Our faith takes hold upon Christ, "who of God is made unto us," not only "wisdom and righteousness," but also "sanctification and redemption."
>
> And what are we to pray for? We are to pray for a supply of all our wants—for pure hearts, and the entire sanctification of our "spirit, soul and body,"—and in a word, for the grace we need to walk in God's commandments, and to do all to his glory. And if

you have attained to the state of entire sanctification, or perfect love, bear in mind, continually, that you are altogether dependent on the efficacy of the blood of Christ, to keep yourself pure and to make advancements in religion. We must likewise pray for our fellow-men—for those embraced in our family-circle, for our relatives, our acquaintances, and for all men, even our enemies. And if our hearts are properly inclined, we are, as a matter of course, interested in the welfare of our fellow-mortals.

Whilst we are desirous to see believers go on to perfection and enjoy the height and depth, and the breadth and the length of the Christian religion, we must ardently pray for the spread of the Gospel and the extension of Christ's kingdom.

WHY IS HOLINESS NOT MORE GENERALLY PREVAILING?

In the MESSENGER of May 8th, 1850, I find the following plain words from this consecrated pen:

"Why is there not more holiness prevailing? Why not more striving after entire sanctification? The principal cause of this great deficiency is, too great neglect of holding up the indispensably necessary doctrine of Christian Perfection. But why is the doctrine of entire sanctification not more generally proclaimed? Because whosoever preaches *perfection* will meet with opposition, not only from non-professors, but likewise from many professors. But there is another reason why this doctrine is not more generally proclaimed, and this is, no doubt, the greatest. There are too many in the field who have themselves not as yet experienced the work—not reached the Canaan of perfect rest, are not striving after it in God's way—and as a natural result, they are incapable to recommend it to others, and to defend the cause in a proper manner. Christ says: 'For out of the abundance of the heart the mouth speaketh.'

"We do not hesitate to allege, that that preacher who has attained and enjoys *the blessing of entire sanctification*, highly appreciates it, and feels it his duty to preach it. Love to God and the Church constrains him to offer this great salvation to his fellow-men, and it is food to his own soul to be engaged in the glorious, work. Even he who has, as yet, not attained *this state of perfection*, but enjoys the witness of his adoption into the family of God, being in the proper light in regard to the subject, and a firm believer in the doctrine, and 'striving lawfully' for the crown, *cannot refrain from proclaiming it* as far as his knowledge relative thereto extends. May the great Head of the Church give the alarm, and send sanctifying grace in copious showers *upon the ministry*—may *preachers and editors* feel the holy fire pervading soul and body, and may we all out of the abundance of our hearts proclaim the good tidings of this full salvation! We may depend upon it, that in order to build up the Church here below—to dress and prepare the stones for the Temple above, where the sound of a hammer will not be heard—*it is as necessary to preach entire sanctification as any other point of doctrine.*

"In conclusion, we would humbly entreat that we endeavor to do all we can to remove all hinderances, that the work of God may take deep root in the hearts of believers generally, and that the Church be not continually troubled with cold professors and backsliders. You that have not attained the state in question, and are not earnestly, perseveringly and believingly striving after holiness of heart and life—after perfect love,—for God's sake be alarmed, and for the sake of your souls, and the souls of your fellow-men, go to work—do not procrastinate—begin to-day, even *now*—read and study the Scriptures, and the sentiments and experiences of such men as

Wesley, Fletcher, Garretson, Bramwell, Carvosso, Albright, Miller, etc. Closely observe all your actions, examine the very intents of your heart, spend much time in secret prayer, endeavor to approach the throne of grace in profound humility, part with every idol, and let Christ empty your heart of all the remains of the carnal mind, and take full possession thereof, to reign there without a rival. Breathe the spirit of prayer at all times, exercise faith in the efficacy of the precious blood of Jesus Christ; strive zealously and manfully; do not be discouraged,, but *look for the blessing—go into it with your whole heart and expect it every hour, yea, even* NOW. If you desire and seek it, it is yours. If you are in possession of it try to walk constantly by faith in the merits of Jesus, living moment by moment. When once the ministry is holy, *then*, generally speaking, we shall have a holy membership."

The following is one of his editorials, in the MESSENGER of 1849:

Much has been said in regard to *entire sanctification* and *Christian perfection*, in both our papers, during the last few months. It has been sufficiently proved that God has provided for the *entire* sanctification of his people in the present life, that he demands such a state, and that he has promised this blessing to all who hunger and thirst for it, and diligently seek it by prayer and faith. But it is not sufficient that we hold to the attainableness of this high state of grace. We believe it, prove it, contend earnestly for it, but alas! how many of us have attained it, or are restlessly pursuing it? Where is the evidence that we are hungering and thirsting after true holiness, and all that mind which was in Christ Jesus—that we expect to be made perfect in love in this life, and that we are groaning after it? These are important inquiries, and they should be duly considered. What can it avail us that God has procured so great a blessing for us, if we do not *enjoy* it? It is a deplorable fact, that in proportion to the number of professors of experimental religion, but very few enjoy entire sanctification. Need we wonder why not more sinners are converted, and that the world, or rather the Church, is filled with backsliders and lukewarm professors? Certainly not. What better thing can be expected, so long as the avowed friends of Christ do not live up to their privileges and duties? But is not the main cause of the want of holiness in the Church to be found with its ministers and official members? Undoubtedly it is.—Well was the injunction given, "Be ye clean that bear the vessels of the Lord." The Church will never take a higher stand in piety than that which the ministry occupies. And the ministry will lead the flock on in the way of holiness in the same proportion in which they are themselves possessed of the spirit of holiness.

The arguments that shall convince, and the words that shall take effect, must come from sanctified lips—must come blazing from a heart itself on fire with heavenly zeal and the love of God.—It is also vastly important that elders and deacons, or class-leaders and exhorters, as well as superintendents and teachers of Sabbath-schools, should be clad with the armor of holiness. Great interests are committed to their trust—they are made, in a measure, responsible for the spiritual improvement and the final salvation of multitudes of souls redeemed by the precious blood of Christ, and, the more deeply they are imbued with the spirit of their Master, the more successfully will they discharge their important trust.—The same may be said of parents and heads of families; and, to a certain extent, of all private Christians. They all have gifts to improve, for the edification of the Church and the benefit of mankind generally.

Then ought not every Christian, particularly every minister and official member of the Church, ask his own conscience the question, *Do I enjoy entire sanctification*? Am I holy in heart and in all manner of conversation? Do I love God with all my heart, and with all my soul, and with all my mind, and my neighbor as myself?

BISHOP SEYBERT'S VOICE

In the *Evangelical Messenger* of July 6, 1871, I find a letter with editorial comments, setting forth the holiness views of this eminent man of God, as follows:

That the first* Bishop of the Evangelical Association was fully in harmony with the doctrine of Entire Sanctification and Christian Perfection, as contained in the Article in our Discipline, seems to be as self-evident as any axiom in science. He dwelt, however, much more upon the experimental and practical aspects than the theoretical, in his advocacy of sanctification, just as does our Article. He preached a thorough, inward and outward, holiness. We heard him once in a sermon, give a criterion whereby a Christian might know that he was entirely sanctified on this wise: "If one who was specially inclined to avarice has, by the help of God, attained a state of grace, which makes him heartily liberal, and induces him to hate even the appearance of stinginess, when he who has been proud, feels such an abhorrence of pride that he goes down a step lower instead of rising up when temptation to pride is offered, etc.; when there is a momentary and perfect victory, with-

---

*The Biographer of Albright shows that Mr. Albright was really the first Bishop. —H.J.B.

out a response from within; when these formerly darling sins are offered, then you may know that you are entirely sanctified." This is a radical definition, but not more so than is the Word of God and genuine experience. A respected friend sent us the following question: "Are there any documents extant, or have we any other reliable sources through which it can be satisfactorily ascertained what were the views of the sainted Bishop Seybert on sanctification and Christians Perfection?" Yes, there are many of them. Perhaps there are none of his testimonies more explicit and positive than a certain correspondence from his pen, published in the *Christliche Botschafter* of July 28th, 1852, of which we here give a faithful translation: "Dear Editor:— My recollection concerning our labors in the East and West Pa. Conferences moves me to the deepest gratitude for the love and friendship, the dear friends manifested toward me while I traveled in these boundaries. And I would remind them to remember what the Lord has done for them during the last conference year, especially in some sections, where moral darkness had been very great. We had such awakenings, revivals, and sound conversions as are seldom seen.

"As a humble co-worker in the vineyard of the Lord, I would fervently exhort the new converts to say with David, from the heart, 'Bless the Lord, O my soul, and forget not all his benefits, who forgiveth all thine iniquities; who healeth all thy diseases.' Imploringly I would also exhort them to die daily unto the world and all evil, deny themselves and take up their cross and follow the Lord Jesus in a holy life; yea, that they may strive in faith with prayer and tears *until their hearts are cleansed from all sin and healed from evil,* and they are fully sanctified through the Divine truth, that they may be enabled with Enoch to walk with God; that is, to live soberly, righteously and godly in this world.

"But this is strange and despised doctrine with the so-called progress of this corrupt age, and the thousands of new-fashioned converts. To be cleansed from all sin, to purify one's self, even as he (Christ) is pure, and then, to live without sin (1 John, 3. 3-9) is carrying the thing too far for most Christians in our days; they hope to get to heaven *without this*. This is the reason why so little fruit of godliness is seen, and the Church is so full of miserable, worldly and backslidden members. These people are only a stumbling block with their profession of Christianity; and this may be the chief cause that infidelity, deism, atheism and universalism make such fearful progress in some places. It is, therefore, *highly necessary*, in my opinion, that all true and faithful ministers and followers of Jesus who see this corruption, insist, with *redoubled earnestness* upon Christian perfection, and especially prove it by their own life and conduct."

These are golden words that ought to be treasured up in every minister's heart. Bishop Seybert did not deal delicately with any remains of sin. He was practical and hesitated not to call that "evil" which is evil, and to say "sin" instead of using frailty, short-comings, faults, weakness, or any palliative and excusing terms, when exposing things that are sinful. He was set against all tinkering of the doctrines of salvation. Especially did he dislike the introduction of the foreign doctrine of sin in the flesh remaining in believers until death. He spoke of this subject in a conversation with us in 1857 in these words: "Oh, I fear this doctrine will do us great harm. If only the dear brethren would seek entire sanctification, instead of commencing to dispute about it."

He was equally opposed to the sentiment that *entire*

sanctification takes place in regeneration, that all of the old man is then entirely cast out so that there are no remains of sin to be removed. The above exhortation given to new converts proves this beyond a doubt, viz: that they should "strive in faith with prayer and tears until *their hearts are cleansed from all sin, and healed from evil,* and they are *fully sanctified* through the Divine truth." (*Dass sie im Glauben mit Gebet und Thraenen ringen mœchten, bis ihre Herzen von allen Suenden rein, vom Uebel geheilt, und sie in der gœttlichen Wahrheit vœllig geheiliget sein mœgen.*)

Have those new converts in the Eastern conferences, to whom this exhortation was addressed, heeded it? Have they sought sanctification "in faith, with prayer and tears?"

The Bishop never changed his theology with reference to this all-important doctrine. Only seventeen days before his death he wrote the following letter to Bro. John Spotts, of Greensburg, Ohio, which is of special interest, both on account of its contents and its being the *last one* he wrote: — "Immanuel—God with us! In great weakness of body, but still fully resolved to serve the Lord and labor in his vineyard to the end of my life, I take my pen to write a little to you, I expect to see you soon and talk with you, the Lord willing. I hope you have not changed in your experience and your principles of religion, with reference to a *lively worship of God and holiness of heart and a holy life.* God help us to stand immovable in all the essentials of the religion of Jesus Christ, and always abound in the work of the Lord, because we know that our labor in the Lord is not in vain. In the neighborhood of ———— things look sad. There the admonition of Christ is applicable, 'Watch and pray, that ye enter not into temptation.' There is little hope for improvement at present, therefore, let him that standeth take heed, lest he fall. But we have still pillars there to support the edifice. Had not the Lord saved a remnant, we would be like Sodom and Gomorrah. To him

alone be honor, praise, glory, and thanksgiving through all eternity. Amen! John Seybert."
"To John Spotts, Dec. 18, 1859."

From this letter it may be seen what deep solicitude the bishop felt in his consecrated heart with reference to changes of views and doctrine. He remained unchanged with regard to holiness of heart and life to the end. His stand-point was the Bible and our Church Discipline, and he ever and always insisted upon the experience and practice of entire holiness as taught in the Oracles of God and by the fathers. Let us follow him as he followed Christ."

A Sermon on Holiness

From the bishop's biography, I translate the following abstract of a sermon preached by him about the year 1849, in a private house in Bucks County, Pa., from the text: *"Blessed and holy is he that hath part in the first resurrection"* Rev. 20. 6. After speaking of the first resurrection, or the millennium, he said, "Blessed and holy is he;" that is, he who has been made spiritually alive, is blessed because he is free from the guilt and the penalty of sin, as the Scriptures say: "Blessed is the man unto whom the Lord imputeth not iniquity." Such a one has remission of sins, and is blessed with the peace of God. But the Holy Spirit has added something else here, namely: *"holy,"* and has firmly bound it with the little conjunction *"and"* to the *"blessed"* so that it is linked together like a chain, which no one can break; for "what God hath joined together, let no man put asunder." He that has been made spiritually alive, has also, in his regeneration, obtained such a measure of the Divine nature and image, that he can have victory over all actual sin, and lead a *holy* life. Now if such person will watch and pray, he can also have dominion over his passions, crucify the old man, and grow up to the stature of

Christian Perfection, in which he will have a holy hatred against all evil, even abhorring his former darling sins; for he possesses power to love God supremely and perfectly. Here, then, love will burn out all envy, pride, worldly fashion, unbelief, avarice, back-biting, and all evil as completely as when natural fire consumes a heap of dry stubble. *That Christian is perfect in love, who, when the devil tempts him to pride, he will get down another degree lower*—when tempted to avarice, he will reach in his pocket and bring an offering unto the Lord; and when he is cursed he will bless in return.

> But the devil has a ministry in the world now-a-days, that will not bear this truth. They admit, since the light shines so clearly, that we must be born again, and they allow also, that we may feel somewhat of the love of God; but no *noise*, nor *shaking* of the dry bones dare take place. These ministers of Satan teach that at best we are always only weak Christians, daily falling into sin, and constantly needing to repent; that we cannot get rid of sin this side of the grave—not till our bodies return to dust. Whoever would be redeemed already in this life from all sin, is branded as being "spiritually proud," "a pharisee," or "self-righteous." Thus the ministry of Satan seeks to tear away the *"holy"* from the *"blessed"*—but the almighty God has put the *"and"* between these two, to hold them together as with a strong clamp or clincher, so that no devil, nor devil's ministry can rend them asunder. *Hallelujah*!
>
> But God also has a ministry in the world, which he himself has called, set apart, anointed with the Holy Ghost, and empowered to preach the whole counsel of God *out of their own experience*. Here the Word of God is preached as it has been learned in the school of Christ. Here *blessedness* and *holiness* united are preached to the people, who are told that *"without holiness* no man shall see the Lord." Here the Word of

God, like a sharp, pointed sword, penetrates and cuts on all sides; for the Word is quick and powerful, and sharper than any two-edged sword, piercing even to the dividing asunder of soul and spirit, and of the joints and marrow, and is a discerner of the thoughts and intents of the heart." Thus we must preach, and thus I intend to preach, until my eyes close in death and my tongue becomes speechless; for the truth must be set upon the throne, and the right hand of the Lord must have the victory!

These blessed and holy ones are the priests of God, and of Christ. By their union with Christ, the eternal High-Priest, they have become a spiritual priesthood, to offer unto God the fruit of their lips, even the sacrifice of praise. They often praise God with a loud voice, giving "glory to God in the highest," or, with the Psalmist, exclaim, "Bless the Lord, O my soul, and forget not all his benefits."

From another sermon preached April 10, 1848, and published in the *Evangelical Messenger* of Sept. 8, 1849, I quote his text with one striking paragraph, as follows:

TEXT—But now being made free from sin, and become servants to God, ye have your fruit unto holiness, and the end everlasting life. For the wages of sin is death; but the gift of God is eternal life, through Jesus Christ our Lord.—Rom. 6. 22, 23.

I wish to say a few words regarding our *"fruit unto holiness:"* As soon as the penitent receives pardon and remission of *all* sins, he is transferred from the service of one master to that of another, freed from the slavery of sin, and engaged in the service of God. Holiness of heart will be his principle, and righteousness of life his fruit.

Brethren and sisters in the Lord, you must be *sanctified*. You must be made pure in heart, or you cannot see God. You must not only abstain from sin, but abhor it. You must maintain the strictest decorum in all your conversation and your dealings. You must glorify God with your spirit, soul and body. Pray to God without delay; delay cannot be any advantage to you, and it might prove the damnation of your immortal souls. Do not, however, be discouraged, Christ is yet on the mercy-seat; and he is willing to fill hungry and panting souls with his gifts. He can prepare your souls *in an instant for the full enjoyment of all the unbounded blessings you may yet need.* The same creating voice that said, "Let there be light, and there was light," can *in the same manner purify and adorn your souls, and make them fit for the presence of the Lord. Then*, my friends, you will be able to bring forth the fruits of the Spirit: love, joy, peace, long-suffering, goodness, meekness and temperance.

Let the reader linger here and take in the full scope of this Episcopal voice, concerning which it has so often been declared that it never gave "a certain sound" on the doctrine of a distinct experience of holiness subsequent to conversion. Who can read the above utterances, and still say, "Bishop Seybert did not teach that we must get entirely sanctified after we have been soundly converted"?

Here is his testimony; and it stands as almost positive proof that if he were living to-day he would be ranked among the so-called holiness preachers.

But I hear still another voice from one who, "though dead, yet he speaketh." It is the familiar voice of

Bishop Joseph Long

In an article written by him in 1869, for the *Living Epistle*, he says:

Holiness is our high calling of God in Christ Jesus, and is absolutely necessary in order that we may answer the end of our being, which is to know, love, obey, enjoy, and glorify God forever.

When God created man he made him in his own likeness; "in the image of God made he him." This, according to the apostle, consisted in knowledge, righteousness, and true holiness. And now, as the Divine Being is infinite, he is neither limited by parts nor definable by passions, and can have no corporeal image after which he made the body of man; hence the image and likeness must necessarily be intellectual; his mind, his soul must have been formed after the nature and perfections of God, who is holy, just, wise, good, and perfect. Such must the soul have been that came from him. There could have been nothing in it, that was impure, unjust, ignorant, evil, low, base, mean, or vile. But man morally considered is not so now; he is fallen, he has lost his glory, he is defiled and corrupt in every part. Yet the counsel of God stands immutable, "and he doeth all his good pleasure" in carding out his wise and gracious plan of salvation. "For this is the will of God, even our Sanctification." Hence he hath chosen us in him (Christ) before the foundation of the world, that we should be holy and without blame before him in love." And, "in the fulness of time," in the gift of his son, who by his obedience, sufferings, and mediation has opened up a new and living way, he made ample provision for the renovation and restoration of fallen man to the image of God, that he might become a fit "habitation of God through the Spirit." This implies justification, regeneration and sanctification.

Sanctification is the work of God's grace by which we are renewed after the image of God and set apart for his service, and it makes us meet for the enjoyment of the presence of God in the kingdom of glory. It must be considered in a twofold light; first, as an inestimable privilege granted us of God; second, as an all-comprehensive duty required of us in his Holy Word. It differs from justification thus:

Justification changes our relation to God as our Judge; Sanctification changes and *purifies our heart to love him as our Father*. In Justification we are saved from the guilt and punishment of sin, and restored to the favor of God; in Sanctification we are saved from the power *and root of sin*, and restored to the image of God.

Sanctification is nothing less than man's entire resignation of his will to the will of God, and to live in the offering up of his soul with all its powers, continually in the flames of love, as a whole burnt-offering to Christ. The grand operating power by which this blessed work is effected is likewise the Divine Spirit, applying the blood of atonement which cleanses us from all sin. But it must be sought by a diligent attendance to all the means of grace, and faithful performance of all the duties enjoined by the Word of God; but above all implicit faith in God "that he is, and that he is a rewarder of them that diligently seek him." It is faith that brings the saving power of God to man, that purifies the heart. *"Thy faith hath saved thee."* And if through faith, then by grace, by the free unmerited mercy of God, as the apostle very elegantly expresses it: "Not by works of righteousness which we have done, but according to his mercy he hath saved us by the washing of regeneration and renewing of the Holy Ghost."

Reader, if thou art justified by faith, and hast peace with God through our Lord Jesus Christ—if thou hast obtained power to become a son of God by receiving the Lord Jesus and believing on his name, *then why tarriest thou short of the full salvation of God*? Arise, and come to the fountain; present yourself a living sacrifice without reserve, soul and body, to God; cast yourself upon the "altar (Christ) which sanctifieth the offering," "that you may be perfect and entire, wanting nothing;" that all "the mind which was in Christ may also be in you," and you be saved from all sin, "that is, from all evil affections and desires," that your heart may be filled with the love of God and man, which is the fulfilment of the whole law, then you will *"be holy as he is holy."* This love is holiness.

These plain and forcible words of the bishop represent him as a very radical holiness teacher, as many now living, well knew him to be. But let us hear him again, as he speaks from the pulpit.

His text is, "In that day there shall be a fountain opened to the house of David and to the inhabitants of Jerusalem for sin and for uncleanness." — Zech. 13. 1.

> Concerning this fountain and its purpose he says: Naturally a *fountain* is a well of water, a useful and living spring. But that the prophet here speaks figuratively and with a spiritual intention, is evident from the spiritual results which are to be produced by this fountain. This fountain alone is the effectual remedy for the "sins and uncleanness" of man. The prophets prophesied under various appropriate figures of the kingdom of Christ and of the Messiah; and to what else could Zachariah refer, when speaking of this fountain, but to the Messiah or the fountain of grace opened by Him for sinners? Christ is an inexhaustible fountain of grace — an *immeasurable fulness*, especially to the house of David and the inhabitants of the *spiritual* Jerusalem; and of "His fulness," says John, "have all we received, and grace for grace."
>
> But that this fountain should be set forth as belonging to the house of David and the inhabitants of Jerusalem, this also must be significant of something more than a literal interpretation. As Abraham and David, with their offspring, had the preference

in the promised Messiah, so also their posterity, as inhabitants, of the earthly Jerusalem, was figurative of the subjects of Christ under the new covenant. Consequently this fountain of Divine grace was not intended for the Jewish nation only, but for the entire Church of the New Testament.

Christ himself appeared on earth, and, as the true substance, put an end to all that was only "a shadow of good things to come;" having pacified the demand of the righteousness of God by satisfying the law— humbling himself that we might be exalted, and becoming poor that we might be rich. He *opened* the fountain through his laborious life and teachings, his patient endurance, and particularly his highly meritorious sufferings and his propitiatory death upon the ignominious cross. To open this fountain wide for us, he sacrificed everything, not even excepting his life. The last drop of his heart's blood was permitted to flow out through the wound made by a soldier's spear. He laid down his life for sinners, that they might be reconciled to God. This, then, was the important "day" when the "house of David and the inhabitants of Jerusalem" could freely drink from the perfectly open fountain. This was the *urgent time*, when the general condition of the world made it necessary that a deliverer should come. It was also a *suitable* time, because the whole world of mankind were languishing in a state of drouth and thirst, the light of the true knowledge of God having been nearly extinguished even among the Jews. "*In that day*" came Jesus with light and grace from God, and opened a free fountain for the refreshing and salvation of the panting multitudes. And, unto *this day*— rejoice all ye sinners!—even *now* the fountain is opened to you through the Gospel.

For us, even *for us*, who hear the Gospel to-day, the fountain of grace stands open, and what else is each

Gospel sermon but a new invitation to share the benefits of this fountain. It is a joyful message, constantly crying: "Ho, every one that thirsteth, come ye to the waters"—"drink without money and without price."

"Be ye reconciled to God."

Ho all ye panting, thirsting souls, do you hear the message—the invitation—the entreaty? It comes to you to-day—the fountain is open to you, open *now*. Not "*in that day*"—not centuries in the future, no, at this time; "now is the day of salvation, now is the accepted time." Oh, then come willingly and in haste to the open fountain! Why do you linger? You are in reach of the fountain, as Hagar was when God opened her eyes so that she saw a well of water. Will you still suffer your soul to languish? The importance of coming to this fountain must appear evident to every one as we further consider *the purpose* for which it was opened. What was the object of opening this fountain at so great a sacrifice? The text says "for sin and uncleanness." This is easily said, but oh, how hard to understand! This fountain is not intended simply to *counterbalance*, but to *overbalance* sin and its effects. It is opened "for (Ger. *against*) sin and uncleanness," so that these cannot affect the fountain, but it is a true antidote against all sin.

What a power, therefore, lies in this fountain! Sins, though numerous and powerful, and uncleanness, though so deep that it permeates the whole man, body and soul, yet these can be removed by this open fountain.

To destroy sin is the purpose for which this fountain has been opened. If there were no sin there would be no guilt and no uncleanness among men, and man would need no pardon and no cleansing. By sin came guilt and punishment upon all men; but Jesus took the punishment upon himself and suffered for them. Sin has polluted all men, but Jesus shed his own blood for their cleansing (1 John 1. 7). Sin plunged all men under the condemnation of death, but Jesus died and brought life for sinners, as it were, out of the dead. He *himself* has therefore become a fountain of grace for us; and he will deliver us from our sins and cleanse us in his blood. Jesus invites all sinners to come unto him, that he may give the thirsty drink, and the weary rest (Matt. 11. 27; John 8. 37). O sinful soul! if thou wouldst be a partaker of salvation, cleansing and refreshing, then comply with the conditions—and you must be a partaker of these or die eternally. Oh, then come with true penitence, come in faith and with sincere longings:—"Ho, every one that thirsteth, come ye to the waters, and he that hath no money, come ye buy, and eat; yea, buy wine and milk without money and without price."

Just at this point my ear has caught the sound of another voice, which has been hushed in death, but not without having left us a definite message on the subject of holiness. It comes from the clear mind and warm heart of one with whom many of us have been familiar. I refer to our beloved brother,

Rev. S.G. Rhoads

His deliverance on the doctrine of Sanctification, as contained in his book, entitled "The Old Way," is clear and strong. Here is what he says in answer to the question:

"What is Sanctification?"

Sanctification denotes in a general sense the ceremonial or ritual consecration of a person or thing to God; but in a particular and doctrinal sense, the making truly and perfectly holy what was before polluted and defiled. To be wholly sanctified means to be saved from all sin; to be pure in heart; to enjoy such a state of Christian experience as to be entirely separated from the world and redeemed from every stain and pollution of sin; so that we live no longer to ourselves, but are wholly consecrated to the service of God.

The doctrine of sanctification, or holiness, is the central idea of revealed religion, and is, therefore, of superior importance. The necessity of holiness is prominently set forth in the Old and New Testament. "And ye shall be unto me a kingdom of priests, and a holy nation." Ex. 19. 6. "For I am the Lord your God: ye shall therefore sanctify yourselves, and ye shall be holy; for I am holy." Lev. 11. 44, 45; Isa. 62. 12. "Let us cleanse ourselves from all filthiness of the flesh and spirit, perfecting holiness in the fear of God." 2 Cor. 7. 1. "For this is the will of God, even your sanctification." 1 Thess. 4. 3. "Follow peace with all men, and holiness, without which no man shall see the Lord." Heb. 12. 14.

The great and glorious object of the advent of the Son of God upon earth was to "destroy the works of the devil" (1 John 3. 8), to "save his people from their sins" (Matt. 1. 21), to "redeem us from all iniquity, and purify unto himself a peculiar people, zealous of good works" (Tit. 2. 14), "that he might present it to himself a glorious Church, not having spot, or wrinkle, or any such thing; but that it should be holy and without blemish." Eph. 5. 27.

It is not only the inestimable privilege, but the solemn and imperative duty of every believer to be entirely holy. Believers must be washed from all the impurities of sin, be cleansed from all filthiness of the flesh and spirit, and be redeemed from every affection and desire, which are contrary to the law and will of God. They are, therefore, commanded to "be holy" (1 Pet. 1. 14-16), to "put off, concerning the former conversation, the old man, which is corrupt according to the deceitful lust" (Eph. 4. 22; Col. 3. 10), to "lay aside every weight, and the sin which doth so easily beset us" (Heb. 12. 1), and "to keep themselves unspotted from the world" (Jas. 1. 27); for no "unclean person hath any inheritance in the kingdom of Christ and of God" (Eph. 5. 5), yea, only the "pure in heart shall see God." Matt. 5. 8.

That there is generally, if not always, something remaining in the believer, after his conversion, that is, that everything is not in perfect order and harmony immediately in regeneration as it should be,— no matter whether that discord, or the cause of it, exists in the spirit, in the soul, or in the body,— and whether we denominate that something, "original sin," "indwelling sin," "moral depravity," "remains of the carnal mind," or by whatever name we please, it is an undeniable fact, it exists somewhere, as frequently indicated in the Word of God, and as verified and corroborated by the almost, if not quite, uniform experience of all believers in every period of the world. But whatever disorder may remain, thank God, there is a "fountain opened to the house of David and the inhabitants of Jerusalem for sin and uncleanness (Zech. 13. 1.), which cleanseth from all pollution; for the Lord is not only willing to pardon sin, when a person comes in the proper disposition of mind and heart, but also to "cleanse from all unrighteousness" (1 John 1. 9),—to "purify the heart" (Acts 15. 9); for "the blood of Jesus Christ the Son of God cleanseth from all sin" (1 John 1. 7); "and every one that hath this hope in him, (of being a Son of God and of being finally glorified), purifieth himself even as he is pure. Whoso committeth sin transgresseth the law; for sin is the transgression of the law. And ye know that he was manifested to take away our sins: and in him is no sin." 1 John 3. 3-5.

After giving denominational testimonies from *nine* different denominations, Mr. Rhoads proceeds to say: In the following particulars all orthodox Christian denominations agree on this doctrine.

First: That man is naturally unholy.

Secondly: That no unholy person can enter into the kingdom of heaven.

Thirdly: That no man can make himself holy.

Fourthly: That the blood of Jesus Christ is the only remedy to make man holy.

Fifthly: That man must be made holy, be entirely sanctified, before he can gain admittance into the presence of God.

All parties, therefore, agree in those points which constitute the most important and essential features, the substance of the doctrine, and the only questions remaining for consideration are, concerning the time and form, when and how it is accomplished. In these respects, I concede, there prevail various and even conflicting opinions among the different denominations, as may be seen in their writings on this subject. With regard to the time, some affirm that it is consummated *immediately before*, or *in death*; others, that it is possible at any time, *long anterior* as well as *immediately before* or *in death*. The latter contend, that, if it is possible for a person to be wholly sanctified one moment prior to death, it is equally possible, days, weeks, months, and even years previously. They say, with God all things are possible. Matt. 19. 26. He is not limited to any particular time, and as He is a perfectly holy Being, and desires that all believers should be entirely holy (1 Pet. 1. 16), not only at some future period, but even *now*, and as He must effect the work, He will accomplish it in every heart, as soon as a person is in the proper state of mind, and complies with the conditions of the Gospel. This view of the subject seems reasonable, and is, in my opinion, correct and Scriptural. It is true, the Holy Scriptures do not specify in so many words, the particular period in which the work is finally consummated: but their whole tenor seems to favor this view.

That entire sanctification may be obtained by every believer, at any time *previous* to death, is quite evident, from the apostle's prayer in behalf of the Thessalonians: "And the very God of peace sanctify you wholly; and I pray God, your whole spirit, and soul, and body, be preserved blameless unto the coming of our Lord Jesus Christ." 1 Thess. 5. 23. We learn from this petition the following particulars:

First: That the Thessalonians, or at least a portion of them, were not *wholly* sanctified.

Secondly: That the Apostle believed that they could be *wholly* sanctified.

Thirdly: That they could be *wholly* sanctified at the time he prayed for them.

Fourthly: That after their *entire* sanctification they could live "blameless" in the sight of God, or how else is the following language to be understood, "Your whole spirit, and soul, and body, *be preserved blameless* unto the coming of our Lord Jesus Christ"?

With regard to the form, the inquiry arises: is sanctification a gradual or instantaneous work? It is, beyond controversy, both. It commences simultaneously with justification and regeneration, and must ultimately, at one period or the other, reach the same perfectness. No one ever obtained entire sanctification in whom it was not previously gradually and progressively developed, to what degree, and for how long a period, I will not presume to specify; and on the other hand, no one ever experienced it gradually, in whom it was not, at one time or another, *instantaneously* consummated. The development is invariably gradual, the consummation *always*, sooner or later, *instantaneous*. In my view, it is entirely unnecessary to dispute about nice distinctions at all. It is of pre-eminent importance, however, that every one should diligently seek with all the heart to be redeemed "wholly" from all remains of the "carnal mind," from "all evil," no matter *how* and *when* it is obtained; but the sooner it is gained the better it is in all respects. Be the change instantaneous or gradual, never rest till it is wrought in your own soul, if you desire to be fully qualified for eternal glory.—

From among the fathers who still linger with us, at the time of this writing, comes the voice of

Rev. W.W. Orwig,

who for years served as Editor of the *Christliche Botschafter*, also as Publishing Agent, and as Bishop. His views, as held in 1869, are stated thus: *Holiness* is the required qualification for God's service and for usefulness in this life, and the only qualification for the inheritance of the saints in light. "Be ye holy, for I am holy," saith the Lord God of hosts. Without holiness none shall see his face.

> Holiness, then, being of such moment to every follower of Jesus, who would not rejoice at every effort put forth for its promotion? In view of this I rejoice in the success of the *Living Epistle*. I trust it will be a powerful means for the promotion of holiness in the Church.
>
> I thank God for sparing me to see the day when so many witnesses in the Evangelical Association testify their belief in, and cherish the doctrine of, Sanctification as taught by the fathers of our Church and expounded in our book of Discipline. *In the early days of my ministerial life this doctrine received much more attention, both by preachers and people than in later years.* At camp and quarterly meetings, particularly, always one or more sermons were preached on holiness, Christian perfection, or perfect love, and frequently with

great effect. There was also much earnest prayer and supplication for the blessing of sanctification, no one supposing that this blessing was generally obtained in conversion. Indeed I never heard this idea advanced in our Church until of late years, although perfect victory over sin, and the possibility of believers living without committing sin, even from the day of their conversion, was always contended for. I shall never forget the power manifested under the preaching of some of the fathers on this subject in my early days; and the effect of those sermons was not merely a surprise at the eloquence of the preacher, but was also practically manifested in the life and devotedness of the members of the Church. Since that time we have had our trials with regard to the glorious doctrine of sanctification; nevertheless *the old standard* is victorious and prevails. The many mighty voices in the Church in favor of it, prove this assertion.

Instructions to Seekers of Entire Sanctification

In his book entitled "Die Heilsfuelle," Bro. Orwig gives directions to seekers, in the following words:

If you need more light on certain points, pray to God for it. If you lack determination, courage and faith, cry to God for help, with the perseverance of Jacob. Unite prayer with searching the Scriptures, and the use of all the means of grace; and employ every help in order to obtain the desired blessing. Besides the Bible, suitable hymns, and verses of hymns, may be a means of encouragement. The reading of books, periodicals, tracts, etc., on the subject may be a help. The Bible, however, must always be considered as the principal source of instruction on this, as on all other points of doctrine respecting our salvation.

Have a single eye, and be sincere before God and man,

in your searchings and prayer with regard to this highly important subject. Conceal nothing, hold nothing back, evade no known duty, spare no passion, renounce every sinful indulgence, remembering that God will not hear us if we regard iniquity in our hearts. We must be conscious that we are sincere before God and man, and that we desire to be saved, and *remain saved* from all sin. If this be the case, then we are only *one* step from the land of entire purity and rest.

But you must consider that without *faith* the specified preparation for sanctification will avail nothing. The most accurate knowledge of the subject, the profoundest sense of our natural depravity and our need of thorough cleansing, all penitence and confession, resignation and consecration, together with the most earnest supplication and prayer, will be without effect if we lack *faith*.

If the proper state of mind is attained, that is, if we have arrived at the borders of the promised land of rest, from internal enemies, and the enjoyment of perfect love—the fulness of God—then it is our privilege by *one further act of faith* to obtain the blessing—to enter into the land and possess it. And this last happy step across the boundary into the promised land, is in most cases not as difficult as many of the preceding steps of our journey have been. We need only to *will* and to *venture*, trusting in the mercy and faithfulness of God, and the work is done. Such faith the Lord requires of all his children, and it is impossible to none.

To believe that God has promised this great blessing, that he is able and willing to impart it, and that he will impart it in due season, is not *all* of that faith which is required to secure the blessing. More is required. We must come, as in justification, to the *present tense*, namely, that he will do it *now*. More than this, that he *actually does it now*. To believe that he will do it is all right at its proper time, but it is not the whole of the requisite faith to secure the blessing. When we believe and feel that we are near the goal, we have achieved a great victory, but if we go no further it will profit us nothing. What would it profit a man if he *almost* came into the possession of a great earthly treasure, or even almost reached heaven, if he finally failed to enjoy it? The application is easy.

All who have been converted or justified, reached a point of time in their penitential struggle, when they by faith obtained the pardon of their sins, and were adopted into the family of God as children. When did they reach that point? Was it not when they *believed*? Not *before*, but as *soon* as they believed. Exactly so it is in the struggle for entire sanctification. The order and nature of faith is the same, the difference is in the object aimed at. In conversion this is justification and regeneration; in sanctification it is entire cleansing from indwelling sin and perfecting in love.

Now if the penitent under the guilt and burden of sin, without much experience in regard to the work and ways of God, may exercise faith to the removal of his sins and obtain peace and consolation, why should he, after such experience and knowledge with regard to the plan of salvation, and God's willingness to hear and answer prayer, not be able to exercise that faith which secures entire purification? Is God not as willing and able to fully sanctify his children as to pardon and renew the penitent? Does he not declare our sanctification to be his will?

We doubt not the fulfilling of a promise made by a well-tried friend—we place full confidence in his word. But our friend is a feeble, fallible mortal, and he might possibly fail to fulfil his promise. He might be overcome by temptation to break his word, or if ever so faithful and willing, not be *able* to fulfil it. But this cannot be the case with God, our best friend. He is immutable, and can in no wise be prevented from fulfilling his promise, if our *unbelief* prevent him not.

But whatever may hinder us and protract our conflict for entire sanctification, the sincere seeker will finally succeed if he persevere. Let him only guard against the mistaken notion that his success lies in the distant future—that weeks, months and even years may pass before he will be able to realize it. This is an artifice of the devil, whereby innumerable multitudes have been deceived. If we earnestly seek the blessing, without which we never shall obtain it, we must expect it *daily, hourly*, yea, *momentarily*. Those who desire more time, have not yet fully discovered their need; are not yet tired enough of inbred sin, and lack earnestness in seeking deliverance therefrom.

Those who hunger and thirst after the full salvation of God, count the days and hours for their deliverance from their inward tormenting foes, and for the full baptism of the Spirit and power of their Redeemer. Deny me what thou wilt, O my God, only not this, is the language of their souls. They willingly consecrate and risk *all* in order to obtain this precious treasure. Nothing on earth or in heaven, seems sufficient to them to mitigate the heart-wound, to fill the heart-void but God and his full salvation. Those who await the blessing in such a frame of mind, and with such a desire by faith, need in no case wait long for it.

If the reader be a seeker of this great salvation, will he permit us to put the following questions to him:

Do you comprehend what is meant by *entire* sanctification? Do you feel the need of it? Do you desire it with all your heart, and are you willing to accept it on any terms? Are you determined to avoid all manner of sin before God and man and to continue in prayer and supplication by faith until you have succeeded? Have you made a full consecration of yourself and yours, your property, your gifts and talents, your time, your influence and honor—your all; and are you determined never to take anything back? Is this your will, your feeling, your determination? Are you resolved to live and die with this mind? Do you expect sanctification by *faith alone*? Do you expect it *to-day, now*? Do you expect it as a work of the Holy Spirit applying the blood of Jesus to your soul? Do you expect with it a fuller baptism of the Holy Ghost than you ever experienced before? Do you expect besides, a cleansing from all inward pollution of sin, an increase of love toward God and man, of spiritual gifts, and an improvement of all the Christian virtues, etc.? All this you may expect with certainty, if you exercise the requisite faith for the attainment of entire sanctification. If you seek it by earnest prayer, and expect it by faith, it must be and will be your portion. Heaven and earth will pass away, but the word and promises of God will remain forever. Do you believe this? "All things are possible to him that believeth." *Do you believe* NOW? If you do you are not disappointed, you have the blessing, and you know and feel it. You need now not be told to give God the glory. The grace of God in your heart will incite you to this. You will speak out of the abundance of the heart, and be constrained to cry out in the language of the Psalmist:

"Bless the Lord, O my soul; and all that is within me, bless his holy name. Bless the Lord, O my soul, and forget not all his benefits: who forgiveth all thine iniquities; who healeth all thy diseases; who redeemeth thy life from destruction; who crowneth thee with loving kindness and tender mercies; who satisfieth thy mouth with good things, so that thy youth is renewed like the eagle's."

JUSTIFICATION, REGENERATION AND SANCTIFICATION

Concerning these doctrines I quote from the same author, as follows: In the glorious and happy state of the justified and regenerated Christian, although he have not yet attained unto entire sanctification, he has forgiveness of his sins, is in possession of peace with God, comfort and joy in the Holy Ghost—is a child of God, and has a right to the heavenly inheritance. The power of sin or of his spiritual malady is broken, and he is placed in a state of spiritual security. The desires, inclinations and emotions of his soul are changed and have been turned in a different direction. The preponderance of the same is against sin and for God. He has power to reign over sin and to lead a holy life.

> But, as in the case of a person recovering from a dangerous bodily malady, although the disease be broken, the pain greatly alleviated and the danger turned away, he is not yet freed from all the symptoms and afterpains of the disease, and not yet fully restored to health; so it is with the Christian recovering from the malady of sin. In justification and regeneration the disorder of the soul, caused by sin, is generally not fully extirpated, the impurity of the disease not entirely purged out. There yet exists some impure moral fluid or ingredient which causes more or less discomfort, and if the proper treatment be neglected, may easily grow worse and frustrate the progress already gained, as is often the case in bodily diseases, followed by sudden death. This ingredient may, by the great change effected in a sound conversion, have been driven in the background, so as not to be apprehended or felt for a while. Or, to speak without a figure, the remaining disorder

of the passions, or the sinful propensities, of whatever kind they may be, as self-love, love of the world, pride, envy, anger, revenge, impatience, etc., may, by the change of the inner man in regeneration, have been so dislodged that they for the time being appear entirely eradicated. Everything in the soul may seem pure and good, and the convert consider himself fully saved from inward as well as from outward sin. But he generally soon discovers his mistake, and finds that the old man—his sinful nature—has not yet fully expired.

True, the guilt of sin is forgiven, its penalty is removed, its power is broken, its dominion has ceased, and the love of sin is rooted out. In a deliverance from sin in justification and regeneration, to such an extent, we believe. But where do we find evidence that every sinful desire, propensity and emotion is *entirely* eradicated in conversion? Or where is it proven that the heart, the mind and the senses—soul and body—are perfectly cleansed from all moral defilement, from every sinful pollution in or at the time of justification and regeneration? That the *entirely sanctified* Christian enjoys such a state of purity, and that it is the duty and privilege of every Christian to attain to such a state we readily admit. But of newly converted Christians, or babes in Christ, such a state of perfection is generally not expected, nor is it proven by the experience of Christians in general.

Nevertheless all are admonished to follow after holiness, without which no man shall see the Lord. How soon after conversion this state of grace may be obtained depends upon the knowledge of its *nature and necessity*, and the *manner* of its attainment, together with the *sincerity* and *earnestness* with which it is sought. Those who seek it by unwavering faith in Christ, will find it. Reader, remember, by FAITH we are *justified, sanctified* and *saved.*—

Another voice, mild, tremulous, but positive, arrests my attention, and as I look I see the slender form and pleasant countenance of

Rev. Charles Hammer

Bro. Hammer was for many years connected with the publishing interests of our Church. As I listen to his voice on the subject of holiness, I hear him in a letter, which he published in 1881, give the following clear statement and testimony:

> In the early part of my ministry in the Evangelical Association I was personally acquainted with all the itinerant ministers of our Church that were then in active service; also with a majority of those that were in active service before my time, but who had already located, either on account of bodily infirmities or family circumstances; and, as far as the fundamental doctrines of our holy religion are concerned, namely the doctrine of original sin, justification by faith, regeneration, and entire sanctification, there was, generally speaking, but one voice. All believed in these fundamental doctrines, and, if any one deviated and preached an erroneous doctrine, he was soon brought to account, and, if he was not willing to recant, he was forthwith silenced. Thus several of our most talented ministers were lost to our Church fifty years ago. There was not that diversity of opinion among us with regard to the doctrine of entire sanctification as there has been since and is at the present time.
>
> Now, I would ask, what is the cause of all this? There is certainly a reason for it. The doctrine of entire sanctification, as it is contained in our Discipline, under the heading, "Christian Perfection," found no opposition among our ministry in the early history of our Church. They believed in the doctrine, advocated it and

labored to lead the believers to that holiness of heart and life without which no man can see the Lord. They studied it as it was taught by the founders of our Church. *They were not ignorant of the experience those holy men of God— namely, Albright, Miller, and others—had with regard to this matter.* Their life had been published, and was read and studied with the greatest interest, both by the ministers and the laity. The doctrine could be preached without offending any, save Satan and his adherents. The result was that not only sinners were converted, but believers sanctified and established upon the Rock of Ages, and thus enabled to endure steadfast unto the end. How different it is now! There is no doctrinal point more discussed in the present age than the doctrine of entire sanctification, and none finds greater opposition, notwithstanding it is one of the most essential and important as well as one of the most glorious doctrines of the Bible. It would seem that, with all the advancement the Church has made since those early days, in this one particular it has been, in a general way, retrograding. If the article on Christian Perfection, as contained in our Church Discipline, were more thoroughly studied by our ministry in general, and an experimental knowledge of it derived by making a full surrender and exercising a living faith in the blood of the atonement, there would certainly be a different state of things in the Church. This Article is clear, sound, logical and Scriptural. If such a course were pursued by all, then the teaching among us would be uniform, as it by all means should be. Our people would not be so apt to get confused with regard to this matter, for they would get all necessary light on the subject, and the battle-cry throughout the whole Church would be, "Onward! Holiness unto the Lord!" Thousands of souls would be saved, who otherwise fall into a state of lethargy, hinder their own usefulness, and lose their souls. What a power the Church would be if all her ministers were clothed with holiness, and were uniform in their teachings concerning this doctrine!

Holiness, Half a Century Ago

At the time I became a member of the Evangelical Association, fifty-six years ago, there was a general longing after purity of heart, at least where I was acquainted. The class to which I belonged, with its leader, was wide awake on the subject. Nearly every member was engaged in seeking the blessing, and among them, also, the writer. A more united effort for full salvation is seldom witnessed than was manifested in this class.

I was afterwards a member of a class in Lebanon, Pa., which was led by Bro. H. Fisher, who, in after years, up to the day of his death, was editor of the *Evangelical Messenger*. He urged the great necessity of seeking holiness of heart and life. *He took the lead and said, "Come" and the flock followed, him, and, oh, what an exemplary class it was*! It is known that Bro. Fisher, in after years, during his ministerial and editorial career, was one of the strongest advocates in the Church of entire sanctification.

It cannot, however, be denied, that, in former as well as in later years, the good work has suffered more or less in consequence of those who made a loud profession, of entire sanctification, but did not live up to it. Their life and conduct did not correspond with their profession. Then others, who had an erroneous conception of the work, went altogether to the other extreme, and thus great injury has been done to the cause. Such characters as above mentioned have always been a stumbling-block in the way, so that weak Christians have been offended and have fallen into skepticism with regard to the doctrine. But is it not great folly to take such characters as examples? Why not look upon Christ and his apostles? Why not look upon such, in our day, as not only profess to have realized the blessing of entire sanctification, but who also manifest in their lives that they are saved—that they are devoted to the Lord—and that it is their meat and drink to do the will of their heavenly Father? Why not take such as examples? Thank God that we are blessed with such, both among the ministry and laity, and they are shining lights in the world, and follow the Lamb whithersoever he goeth. May the number increase, and the work of holiness spread throughout the length and breadth of our Church.

These are plain and valuable words from one whose whole life has been devoted to the interests of his Church in the furtherance of Christ's cause; and who always speaks soberly and thoughtfully.

Let us hear him further. In 1874, he wrote as follows:

...The doctrine of entire sanctification, or holiness of heart and life, is certainly no new doctrine among us. I have the honor of having been a member for nearly fifty years, and have served God and the Church, in a public capacity, for the last forty-five years, and I can testify to the fact that this doctrine was preached and practiced when I first became a member. I may also add that I never heard it preached with more power and demonstration of the Spirit than I did then. It also had a wonderful effect, so that members were engaged in seeking the blessing, with whom, thank God, the writer took an active part, even before he entered upon his public ministrations. Many also realized the blessing, who have long since gone to their eternal home, while others are still faithfully moving onward, soon to strike the other shore.

ERRORS AND THEIR EFFECTS

I admit that from the year 1833, or 1834, the same attention was not paid to the subject as before, or as has been the case within the last fifteen or twenty years. I might give various reasons for this, but will merely give what I consider the most prominent one. The matter had been carried altogether to extremes by many of the advocates of holiness, and the consequence was, that some had fallen into gross errors and brought reproach upon the good cause.

One of these errors was, that a wholly sanctified person could not sin any more, he was out of danger; Satan had lost his power forever over him. The language of one to me, was, "I can never fall into sin, I am wholly sanctified, I am always happy, my eternal salvation is sealed." This was an elderly person of considerable experience and influence, and it was only one out of many that had fallen into this great error. Besides this, some had become real fanatics; many left the Church, and others had to be expelled.

The result was that the Church had, more or less, fallen into the other extreme, so that for some years the subject was not agitated, and impressed upon the minds of believers as it should have been, although, as a general thing, the whole counsel of God was preached by our ministers, and that with good success.

From the above facts we may learn how necessary it is that we guard against extremes in any doctrinal point. Experience has taught us that if people get too much excited on the subject of holiness (or any other subject. H.J.B.), they are in great danger of going to extremes; but there is also great danger of professors of religion being too indifferent with regard to this important matter. No wonder that so many do not enjoy themselves in the sweet comforts of our holy religion as they should; yea, no wonder that so many backslide after having found Jesus precious to their souls.

[It is a great pity, indeed, that "errors," "extremes," and "fanaticism," should ever creep into any movement that is devoted to the spread of holiness; but such is often the case, and, while these evils must be pointed out, and guarded against, they furnish no excuse whatever for neglecting the duty of striving after perfect love, and of urging believers to become partakers of the same, H.J.B.]

THE NEW CONVERT'S FIRST DUTY

The first thing to be considered by the new convert, ought to be, How may I now be cleansed from inward corruption, and made holy in heart and life? How may I make a full and entire consecration, so as to be wholly devoted to the Lord? How may I attain to that higher state in the Christian life, in which I may be able to love the Lord with all my heart, soul, mind, might and strength, and my neighbor as myself? How may I become useful and exert a good and wholesome influence among my fellow-men?

Such, or like questions ought to be made, not only by converts, but also by old professors who are not in possession of entire sanctification; *and, at the same time proper efforts should be made to obtain the blessing*. If this was the case there would not be so much backsliding, not so much worldly-mindedness, nor indifference about religion, not so much fault-finding and criticism with regard to the subject of sanctification. Oh, what a blessing it would be if all, preachers and people, would take the above course! Then there would be unity of spirit and sentiment among us, and discussions on the subject of holiness would cease; perfect love would rule and reign within us, and we would be wholly the Lord's... We have great reason to be thankful to God that our Church has been waked up on this subject, and within the last few years more so than ever before, and I trust the good work will go on and continue to spread until the holy fire shall burn throughout the length and breadth of the entire Church.

How Entire Sanctification is Obtained

I wish yet to touch on a point connected with the above, which I consider of great importance, and that is, the manner in which the blessing of entire sanctification is obtained. It is said to be obtained through faith; that we must believe, etc. Now this I will not dispute, but the question is, Who is it that *can* believe? Who is it that *can* lay hold of God's promises, by faith, and say, It will and must be done? Certainly not the one who has not a proper knowledge of himself and his inward depravity. I have frequently heard sermons on the subject of sanctification, in which but very little if anything was said on this point.

I once attended a series of holiness meetings which were conducted by two prominent, and no doubt, holy persons. There was much said that was very good, but very little of the preparation of heart necessary, in order to have the blood of Christ applied to a thorough cleansing. Professors were invited forward to the altar, and many came, evening after evening. It was impressed upon them to believe, to exercise faith, etc., and a number professed to have found the blessing. But in my estimation the work was too superficial, because of a want of a proper preparation of heart to make a complete surrender. *In my estimation it is just as nec-*

essary for a believer to know and to feel his inward depravity, in order to be able to give himself wholly to the Lord, and to have the blood of Christ applied by faith, to the cleansing of his heart, as it is for the sinner to know and to feel his sins, in order to believe and to find pardon.

Premature Professions

It is a lamentable fact that the cause has suffered much on account of so many that made a loud profession of entire sanctification when they had only learned the first principles of the Christian religion. There is no consistency in making such a profession as long as unbelief, pride, anger, self-will, envy, coveteousness, worldly-mindedness, etc., show themselves, and have the ascendency [sic], or when there is no fervency, unction, or power in our public exercises, as in praying, exhorting, preaching, etc.,—when we are wavering, not established, weak in faith, without a burning zeal for God, and for the salvation of mankind. As long as we are thus defective, we ought not to make any pretensions to having attained to a higher state in the Christian life. We must know and feel our unworthiness, our entire nothingness, the stains which sin has left within us; the sin which doth so easily beset us. In order to obtain this knowledge, it is necessary, often, to look into the depths of our hearts, and at the same time ask God in fervent prayer for light and understanding. Sometimes it is even necessary to take recourse to abstinence, and to fasting. Whoever pursues this course will sooner or later be prepared to plunge into the fountain filled with blood, he being willing to give up all for Christ, to lay all upon the altar, and then take hold, by faith, of God's promises, and thus the work will be completed. God will do it by the operation of his Holy Spirit; then we will be holy in all manner of conversation, fully possessed of God and his love, and show by our walk and conduct, and by all we do that we are the Lord's.

Then let us proclaim to all around us what the Lord has done for us, and we shall bring honor to the doctrine, and to the cause of Christ in general.

In conclusion I would yet add that *no minister of the Gospel can do the work fully which God has assigned him unless he enjoys the blessing of entire sanctification. Neither can any professed Christian live fully in accordance with the teachings of our blessed Saviour and his apostles without it.* Now since this is a fact which cannot be denied, let all obey the divine injunction: "Follow peace with all men, and holiness, without which no man shall see the Lord."

I have taken the liberty to italicise a few sentences, order to fix the attention of the reader upon these striking points which deserve more than a mere passing notice.

I next introduce from the pen of Father Hammer a brief sketch of

REV. JACOB SCHNERR

and his relation to the holiness work. The writer says: Rev. Jacob Schnerr, who labored with great success as an itinerant preacher, among us, from 1829 to 1838, when his health failed, was not only a holy and devoted man of God himself, but he also preached holiness of heart and life, and urged the believers to seek this inestimable blessing without delay. Concerning this work I here give a few items from his own journal. At one place he writes of a powerful meeting which he had August 20, 1833, at Lebanon, Pa. On this occasion he preached from this text; "Is not my word like as a fire? saith the Lord; and like a hammer that breaketh the rock in pieces?" Jer. 23. 29. The following day he conducted a class meeting, of which he says: "It was a wonderful time." He there urged the necessity of entire sanctification, and, "quite a number engaged in seeking the blessing, some of whom found it during that service;" and of others he says, "I hope they will continue their pursuit of it, until they also realize the cleansing power of Jesus' blood."

At another time, on this same circuit, he came to a place where we had a flourishing society, but a number of the members had fallen into great errors regarding the doctrine of entire sanctification. It grieved Bro. Schnerr very much when he learned this fact. So he visited them and tried his utmost to convince them of their errors, but he could do nothing with them. Then he said, "There is no other way, I must *preach* on the subject. This he did, and his sermon seems to have been very powerful and convincing, for these errorists could not withstand it. "They yielded, and were set right again."

He did not then, on account of the errors into which some had fallen, cease to preach and urge the people forward to holiness, but having exposed their errors, he says he "urged the necessity of seeking the blessing of sanctification." Father Hammer closes this sketch by saying, "Many instances might be mentioned of his wonderful success in building up the cause of Christ; but those already mentioned will serve to show that he was an advocate of the doctrine of holiness."

It is worthy of note that the methods of this remarkable man of God were very much like those employed at present by the so-called holiness people. He urged the people at once to seek entire sanctification, and to seek *until they realized it.*

III
THE VOICE OF THE PRESS

IN SPEAKING OF THE VOICE of the press I refer especially to the periodical publications of the Evangelical Association, through which most of the voices that speak in this book first came to our ears.

Many excellent things have been said on the subject of holiness, through the *Evangelical Messenger*, and the *Christliche Botschafter*. And, some of our best selections have been gathered from these great and influential Church organs.

But it is well known that the Evangelical Association has taken a step in advance of her sister denominations in publishing a special Holiness Periodical as *An Official Organ*.

This magazine—*The Living Epistle*—was founded in 1869 by several brethren who felt called to do something special to help forward the great holiness movement," which begun about that time to make itself felt in the Churches.

After a successful career of nearly three years, under the management of its founders, the General Conference assembled, at Naperville, Ill., in the month of October, A.D. 1871, purchased this monthly, and elected an editor for it. This was done, with a thorough knowledge of the radical character of its teachings on holiness. The editor then elected (Rev. Jacob Young) was also known to the Church as a radical teacher, and a professor of holiness. Thus the Church opened a new channel for the spreading of Scriptural holiness—a channel through which the voice of definite holiness teaching and testimony has been heard by thousands, and made an inexpressible blessing to hundreds, if not thousands.

The reader will, therefore, pardon the frequent allusions to, and the numerous quotations from, this source, inasmuch as it contains so many of the deliverances of the Church on the all-important subject of Entire Sanctification.

Besides the periodicals already mentioned, I have drawn also from the *Evangelische Magazin*, which, during its first years was not a general Family Magazine as it now is, having been more especially devoted to theology. The first and second volumes of this excellent Monthly give great prominence to the subject of holiness, both editorially, and through some of its contributors. A free translation of some of these editorials and articles is given in connection with other selections as from "The Voice of the Press."

The voices to which the reader's attention is called, are chiefly from those loyal leaders in the Church, whose ability, orthodoxy, and faithfulness have secured them the highest positions among us, and who have spoken freely on this subject, through the press.

The name of Bishop J. J. Esher has already been introduced to the reader, in connection with his comments on our formulated statements of the doctrine of holiness, and his authorship of the new edition of our Catechism. But we must let him speak again, for he generally speaks wisely and well.

Of him Rev. W. W. Orwig wrote thus, in 1873:— "As to doctrine, the bishop is *eminently orthodox* according to the creed of his Church, and he has, since his connection with it, always been a believer and a defender of the doctrine of *holiness* and *Christian perfection* as held by it. Of late years, particularly has he preached much on entire consecration and sanctification, to the edification and encouragement of all who were in sympathy with the *glorious holiness movement* of our time, and with holiness in general."

From the Bishop's pen I find the following, published in 1869:—

Sanctification—Its Condition

Our sanctification is of God; it is founded in his being and will, and he is its source. His word commands it, and teaches what it is. Christ, who by his sacrificial death and his resurrection and glorification, is the meritorious and mediatorial cause, the author of our sanctification, in his life upon earth, sets before us a real, life-like and perfect model of that holiness to which we, his followers, are called according to the will of God, which is our sanctification, wrought and established in us in divine reality by the Holy Spirit, who filleth us with the life, and light, and love of God.

Being created in the image of God, we are susceptible of his life and his holiness. Corruption entered by the fall, but by the renewing wrought by the Holy Spirit in us in our regeneration, by which we pass from death unto life, the new life-foundation of our entire sanctification and perfect holiness is laid in our hearts. Our sins are forgiven, and we are saved from the power and dominion of sin, standing in the grace of the new life, and walking in the light of the living God, and our Saviour, Jesus Christ; in which light we know ourselves now as we could not know ourselves before regeneration. But we likewise know the will of God and the riches of the grace of our Lord Jesus Christ, with a far clearer knowledge than previous to our being brought from darkness into his marvelous light.

Concomitant with this superior knowledge is the longing, earnest desire of the renewed believer to be the Lord's only, and to be his entirely and forever—to be made holy even as God, the object of his supreme love, is holy; and to live in righteousness and holiness as it is pleasing in the sight of Him who hates every impurity and evil. In this knowledge, rooted in the experience of the new life, faith rises with a certainty and might such as was absolutely impossible before conversion. And thus the believer attains to that higher state of grace and divine life which is known as entire sanctification and Christian perfection, and implies:

1. An entire separation from sin; the purification, by the blood of Jesus, from all evil affections and desires included.

2. Being filled, spirit, soul and body, with the love of God, the same quickening all the powers of life in us for the service of Christ, governing our mind, will and affections, filling the mind with the light of the glory of God in the face of Jesus Christ, and the will with delight and strength for the service of the Lord, and the affections with heavenly desires and enjoyment, so that we wholly live in God, and he in us.

3. Connected with this inner holy state is a like holy practice in life, a godly walk and conversation, following Christ in his footsteps, yea, *in his footsteps*, and this not imaginarily but in reality, doing and suffering the will of God even as he did, still rising higher in this entire communion with God.

Consecration and Faith

The means by which we obtain this blessing—for a blessing it is, the gift of God by grace—is simply that faith which sees all this in Christ Jesus, and expects it momentarily from him as a perfect Redeemer; provided, however, that the consecration which we have vowed in our repentance, and exercised as far as we had knowledge, has been steadfastly and faithfully practiced in the light which was given us, and as the light in which the believer stands is so much clearer and stronger than that of the penitent sinner, so likewise is the consecration with which the believer offers himself to God much more comprehensive, pure, intense and entire than that of the repenting sinner possibly could be. His surrender was more of fear, the thunders of Sinai chasing him, but the believer's consecration is *that of love*—of that love which would live and die for Jesus. The love which the Holy Ghost kindled in regeneration is the strong motive power which urges us almost irresistibly to lay ourselves upon the altar of Christ as a burnt-offering for the Holy One in Israel. This consecration of the believer is, indeed, the result of, and, therefore, similar to that of the penitent; but it is at the same time different, for if it possesses the same elements, it certainly has them in a vastly different proportion. The believer's sacrifice is emphatically a sacrifice of love, a desire of love, to love perfectly, a giving away of self by love, and a taking by that faith which reaches into the riches of Christ just so deep as the desire of the soul penetrates.

He that gives himself thus to Christ and takes the offered treasures of grace in such a manner, will be filled with all the fulness of God, and transformed into the image of Christ, whose he is, "from glory to glory, even as by the Spirit of the Lord."

Experimental and Practical Holiness

Under this title I find the following from the pen of R. Yeakel:— Christian Holiness is eminently experimental and practical. If we separate experience and practice, or substitute mere theory, we have but a miserable deformity. He who would have inward experience only is an enthusiast, and he who would have practice only, is a pharisee, and the theorist deals in empty words and speculations. Holiness deals with facts and realities; it is a *living truth*— Christ the eternal Truth, who is our Sanctification, dwelling constantly in the heart by faith, and governing the *whole life*. Holiness does not spin cob-webs over our sin and depravity, but searches and reveals those things to their very depth as they are seen of God, and brings in Christ the mighty Sanctifier. The apostles of our Lord, who graduated in the school of Christ himself, and hence were master "Doctors of Divinity" treated this subject in a very *practical* way. They were "full of faith and the Holy Ghost," and apprehended the real condition of individuals and of churches under their care, not by superfine speculations and theories, but simply by looking at things in the light of God, as they were. And what did they see among the Christians? They saw all the good already wrought in and among them, with grateful ascriptions of praise to God; but they also saw that there was much carnality existing among believers, manifesting itself in "envyings, strife, and divisions;" that some who "for the time ought to be teachers," needed again "to lay the foundation," and that others conducted themselves in a manner not worthy of their high calling in Christ Jesus. This fact was so palpable that Paul feared he would find some of the churches far below the standard of holiness.—"For I fear, lest when I come, I shall not find you such as I would, and that I shall be found unto you, such as you would not; lest there be debates, envyings, wraths, strifes, backbitings, whisperings, swellings, tumults." The apostles deeply and sorrowfully felt the stubborn fact that there was a *great want of holiness* among believers, and as sensible and practical men they accepted it as a fact, and labored accordingly, to remedy the evil. They did not spend either strength or time in critical discussions and disputes about the *location, extent*, etc., of the depravity in believers, or how it came there; nor did they stop to split hairs about its gradual or instantaneous extirpation, but went straight at it. Hence they were very emphatic in telling believers that those remains of evil were contrary to the truth as it is in Jesus, and insisted upon the utter eradication of all that was sinful, or had even the appearance of evil. They earnestly entreated them to "put off the old man," and to "cleanse themselves from all filthiness of the flesh and spirit, *perfecting holiness* in the fear of God;" so that they might "present every man perfect in Christ Jesus," and bring the Church a spotless bride into the presence of Christ.

> On the other hand, they offered and proclaimed *Christ* to believers as the *only* and *all-sufficient* source and fountain of holiness—"who gave himself for the Church that he might *cleanse it*;"—"who of God is made unto us *Sanctification"*—whose blood "cleanseth *from all sin*;" asserting at the same time: "This is the will of God, *even your Sanctification*," and praying: "The very God of peace sanctify you *wholly*; and I pray God your whole spirit, soul, and body, be preserved blameless unto the coming of our Lord Jesus Christ." They required of believers a total separation from all evil, the mortification and death of the old man, and unreserved submission to him who died for them and rose again that they might live a life of *continual faith* and *perfect holiness*. These eminent men of God were earnest practical, holy Radicals, uncompromisingly attacking the

"last and least remains of sin" wherever found among believers, and insisting on salvation "to the *uttermost!*"

Paul, who was himself a living example of entire holiness and Christian perfection, presented his own experience and state of grace, before his erring Galatian brethren in the following unsurpassable confession: "I am crucified with Christ, nevertheless I live; yet not I, but Christ liveth in me; and the life that I now live in the flesh, I live by the faith of the Son of God, who loved me and gave himself for me." Gal. 2. 20. Here we have Christian holiness and perfection as *realized* by Paul, and urged by him in his writings and preaching, and boldly professed for an example to them that should believe. Here is no supposition, superficial feeling, "vain babbling," speculative theory, nor labyrinth of unwarranted inferences which confuse the mind and discourage the heart, but a *live man filled and governed by Christ*, who can positively and truthfully assert: "*I can do all things* through Christ, who strengthened me." How simple and clear, and yet how sublime and powerful is this confession! Being *crucified with Christ*, the *death of the selfish self*, and the *full life of Christ within* were in Paul practical, radical—we might almost say, *tangible* realities! Most glorious fact! May it be repeated in all preachers of the Gospel and professors of Christianity!

And now we would ask in all seriousness: Is there any other holiness or any way of obtaining it except this thorough, old Evangelical and Apostolical, practical one, that will answer the purpose? Or is indeed, in our day of spiritual superficially "the congregation holy, *every one of them*?"— as the rebels Korah, Dathan and Abiram said to Moses with reference to the stiff-necked people of Israel. Far from it. Is there a true servant of Christ who does not to his heart's sorrow perceive the great want of holiness in the Church? How prevalent are doubt and unbelief; how distressing envyings and strife; how rampant the weeds of pride and fashion; how mighty is the detestable spirit of avarice, and how much lukewarmness and conformity to the maxims of the world prevail; what alacrity to respond to the calls of the so-called innocent worldly amusements, and what hesitancy to discharge duty, even the highest privileges of the Christian being regarded as *crosses*! Very few can truly say: "Not I, but Christ liveth in me." Who will deny these facts? They exist, they confront us at every turn, and, as it were, strike into our faces and sting our very hearts! They are the greatest obstacles to Christ's cause, eating out the vitals and crippling the energies of the Church to a fearful degree.

But, though we have the same want of holiness to deplore as the apostles had in their time, yet, thank God, we have the same overflowing fountain of holiness and grace—"Jesus Christ, the same yesterday, today, and forever!" Now this great want of holiness in believers, is one fact, and Christ made unto them sanctification, is the other fact with which we have to do. We must accept these facts as they are, because *they are facts*.

How to Get Believers Sanctified

A practical way of preaching which faithfully attacks, exposes, and reproves the depravities existing in the Church, and at the same time leads believers directly into the fulness of Christ's free, full and present salvation, is the great desideratum. Such preaching will induce many believers to wash their robes *white* in the blood of the Lamb. This will effect infinitely more than all the discussions concerning the supposed critical niceties of the doctrine of Sanctification have ever effected. If we thus preach, the Holy Spirit—which is the spirit of truth, will bless our preaching with *dem-*

onstration and *power*. This Great Teacher will reveal to believers their want of holiness and the overflowing fountain of Grace, and as they consecrate themselves entirely, and trust implicitly in Christ, they will find the Entire Sanctification of spirit, soul, and body.

As holiness is an *experimental* and *practical* truth, it is evident that ambassadors for Christ must preach it, not only theoretically, from the Bible, but experimentally from the heart, and practically in their lives. They must be able to stand up and say with Paul: "Follow me, *as I follow Christ.*" This gives almost irresistible force to preaching, and supplies an influence that nothing else can give.

Brethren in the Gospel! We have neither the right to neglect this doctrine, nor yet to preach it according to speculative notions. Let us, therefore, go down to the feet of our Great Master, and thence, with hearts "full of faith and the Holy Ghost" before the people; and let us preach the good old evangelical, apostolical, practical sanctification doctrine, and never beat the air with criticisms, objections, hair-splittings, and polemical metaphysical, high-sounding, but empty, and worse than worthless phrases!

From such Scriptural labors will result a Church wholly devoted to God, full of the fruits of the Spirit, and zealous unto all good works, and an invincible power for the conversion of the world.

HOLINESS BEGUN

Those who profess to have obtained a definite experience of holiness, subsequent to conversion, have, by some, been charged with ignoring the fact that at conversion we are in any sense made holy. Indeed, I once heard an old veteran in the ministry give this "man of straw" a real sound theological flogging. Now the truth of the matter is, that no one among us has ever taught that we are in no degree sanctified at the time of our regeneration; but we teach that in conversion holiness is *begun*, and that he who "begun this good work" in us will also *perfect* it sooner or later, "if we walk in the light, as he is the light."

The work of grace in its various operations and sanctifying effects, is very clearly set forth in a series of editorials, which appeared in the *Living Epistle* during the editorship of my worthy predecessor, Rev. Jacob Young, from whom I next quote. On the subject of conversion which he sets forth as the beginning of holiness in us, he says:

The term conversion is sometimes used in a limited sense, in which it has different significations; but usually, in a general sense, denoting a radical change of moral character, consisting in the renovation of the heart and life, or a turning from the power of sin and Satan unto God (Acts 26. 18), produced by the influence of Divine grace. Thus used, it includes repentance, justification, regeneration, or the new birth, adoption, the Spirit's witness, *and the work of holiness begun*. This we conceive to be the broad evangelical sense of the comprehensive term "conversion."

In that individual who has received justification, experienced regeneration, be adopted into God's family, and received the Spirit's witness, the work of holiness is begun. The foundation of sanctification is laid. It is impossible to receive the Spirit of adoption without the beginning of the work of holiness.

When these different terms are used in connection with each other, in a limited sense, they have their specific significations, and each of them has reference to a special part of the work of grace in the heart. Then they mean different things, though inseparably connected. Justification and regeneration are then not one and the same thing, but these terms convey two distinct ideas. The term conversion includes them all. But these terms are not always used in this sense. They are frequently used with a more comprehensive signification, including the concomitants. This is the case especially with the term "justification." When used in a general sense, it includes regeneration, adoption, the Spirit's witness and sanctification begun, because they are inseparably connected. The same is true of the term regeneration, and for the same reason.

Conversion, justification, and regeneration, are not unfrequently used synonymously each including the others; being used to convey the same idea as the term *conversion* defined above. They have reference to the same work of grace in the heart, which in all cases includes the work of holiness *begun*, but not necessarily *completed*. Hence when the expressions, justification, justified, or *merely* justified; regeneration, regenerated, or *merely* regenerated are used, it does not follow, nor can it be legitimately inferred, that they are so used to convey the idea that the work of holiness is not begun, unless it is distinctly specified, because they are, generally, if not universally used to designate *conversion*, which includes holiness begun. But why use the term *"merely"*? Simply to make the distinction between the converted, who are *not* yet wholly sanctified, and the converted who *are* wholly sanctified. All the wholly sanctified are justified, regenerated — converted; but not all the converted are wholly sanctified. In a *"merely"* justified, a *"merely"* regenerated — a *"merely"* converted man, the work of sanctification is begun, but not completed. The work of conversion is complete, but a perfect conversion is not entire sanctification.

With the most distinct conception of each as a part of the whole, we do not conceive that one takes place without the other. He that is justified is regenerated—is converted.

Conversion is a glorious change from darkness to light, from death unto life, from the bondage of sin to the liberty of God's children, from nature to grace. The Spirit of adoption is given, and we are made heirs of glory. No wonder the poet sings:—

"How happy every child of grace,
　Who knows his sins forgiven!
This earth, he cries, is not my place,
　I seek my place in heaven."

Again he writes: A conversion which does not affect our life is worth nothing. Our sins being forgiven we must live without committing sin, if we would preserve our justification untarnished. The Scriptures are very definite in requiring of those born of God to live without sinning, i.e. without committing sin. He that sinneth—commits sin—is of the devil. We can not allow ourselves to commit the least sin, or do any wrong act, not even on the ground that we are as yet not wholly sanctified, without falling under condemnation; for it is the privilege and duty of every child of God to live without committing ONE SIN, from the moment of justification to the hour of death. This must be the case if we would remain in a fully justified state. We dare not aim at anything lower than this. We do not say that this *is* the universal or even general experience of the justified; but it *should* be. However many, or few, may fail in this, they in so far tarnish their justification, and need restoration. If the converted allow themselves anything, concerning the right or propriety of which they have doubts, be it in regard to the wearing of gaudy, fashionable, or costly apparel, jewelry, etc.; or concerning amusements, diversions, associations, habits, indulgences, etc., it will dim the evidence of their justification, and cast a gloom, to say the very least, over their religious enjoyment. How many struggle right here, for a season, then compromise, lose the clear assurance of their acceptance with God, and speedily also their justification, sink into a state of formality, passing for Christians—perhaps *good* Christians—while they are backslidden in heart. To say that such are in a justified state would be lowering the Scriptural standard of Justification.

> Nor can the state of justification be retained any considerable length of time, without seeking entire sanctification. It must be the aim of every believer to be pure in heart. As soon as the converted realize that there are remains of the carnal mind, "inbred sin," "evil affections and desires" still in the heart, they must seek cleansing from the same, or they will fall under condemnation. Not indeed from the fact of the presence of "inbred sin," in the heart, but from the fact that they do not seek deliverance therefrom. We dare not remain indifferent in regard to these remains, but must keep them subdued, and seek entire cleansing from them in order to make progress in the divine life, or even to continue in the state of justification. As long as we keep them subdued, holding power over them, fighting against and seeking deliverance from them, we do not fall under condemnation, and will soon experience that "the blood of Jesus Christ His Son cleanseth us from all sin."
>
> We see the folly, then, of excusing anything that is not right, little sins, little evils, etc., as they are generally termed, on the ground that we do not profess holiness. And yet how many, when their attention is called to these things, admit that they are wrong, and add that they know they are not what they ought to be, not right; but they think it covers the whole ground to say: "I don't profess entire sanctification." As much as to say, We are at liberty to do

some things which are not right, as long as we do not profess to be wholly sanctified, and can still be in a justified state.

Remember, if you allow yourself anything which you condemn in those who profess sanctification, you fall under condemnation, seeing you do the very things which you condemn in others. Do not some hesitate to seek entire sanctification, from the fact that they think more would be required of them if they did so? What a sad lowering of the standard! Just as if it were not the duty of every child of God to perfect holiness in the fear of God! To think that you can retain your justification, and make advancement in the divine life without seeking entire sanctification, is most disastrous! The mark must not be lower than the cleansing from all sin, inwardly as well as outwardly.

Thus it is evident that the standard of justification is a high one, and yet we dare not rest here. There is still more to be experienced—a cleansing from all moral defilement. Justification may be complete, and yet "inbred sin," "evil affections and desires" remain in the heart; we must, however, not tolerate or allow them there, but war against them, and not rest till they are completely eradicated.

How very few, comparatively, of those who have been justified freely, measure up to the true standard of justification, continually. Some recede from it and live in a partially or wholly backslidden state. Others frequently yield to temptation, or are overcome by the "evil affections and desires" still remaining in the heart, repent, ask forgiveness, in so far as they have yielded, and are restored, and with them it is, much of the time, up and down, up and down. Some, perhaps the majority, of those belonging to this class, pass for exemplary Christians; but they and their God know how often they yield in their heart, and are restored? Could we see the closet scenes as God sees them, it would astonish us. After yielding to a greater or lesser extent, should we not repent and be restored? Certainly! It is the best thing that can be done, and the sooner the better. How many instead of measuring up to the true standard and full enjoyment of justification, *drag* along heavily, and live at the "poor dying rate," trying to bring the standard down to their experience, instead of bringing their experience up to the standard.

The man that lives up to the full measure of justification is a happy being. Faithfulness will increase his happiness. If all those who profess the religion of Jesus measured up to the true standard of conversion, in experience and practice, what a stir it would make in the Christian world! How easily, comparatively, believers might be led on to the experience of perfect purity through the blood of the Lamb. What multitudes would be wholly sanctified! What crowds of sinners would be brought to Jesus!

What Bro. Y. here plainly and correctly teaches may be summed up thus: As soon as holiness is begun in us, by regeneration, we are saved from *sinning*, though not necessarily from *sin*, in the sense of its inbeing, as a root from which there is a tendency to evil productions. But *sinning* must and does cease at conversion, and *holiness begins.—*

Sin in Believers

The same writer, at a later date, gives his views on "sin in believers," in the following language:

"Sin is the transgression of the law." "All unrighteousness is sin." "Whosoever doeth not righteousness is not of God." Not only the outward act of transgression, but all nonconformity to, and deviation from, the law of God is sin. There is original sin and actual sin. The Bible teaches that there is sinful depravity—inbred sin—and it also speaks of open violation of God's law.

There is no dispute on the question of sin in the *unconverted*, but the question of sin in *believers* is not so fully settled in every mind. That in conversion we are saved from outward or actual sin, and that we must live without *committing* sin, dare not even allow or tolerate sin, if we would retain our justification, admits of no doubt; but it must also be admitted that the converted, generally speaking, sooner or later, if they are faithful, realize that there are "affections, desires," etc., in their hearts, which are not in conformity with the law and nature of God. Some do not like to apply the name sin to anything which still remains in the heart of the truly converted; perhaps they in their minds associate it too much with the idea of actual sin.

It is generally held that conversion is not entire sanctification, and that there are *remains* from which we must be saved after conversion. To these remains various appellations have been given; such as "evil heart," "inward foes," "inward evils," "corrupt nature," "remains of the carnal mind," "the old man," "moral depravity or corruption," "remains of sin," "indwelling sin," "inward sin," "inbred sin," "inbeing of sin," "original sin," etc. In some of these terms the word sin is not used; in others it is. The more I study the subject the more I am convinced that it is proper to say remains of sin, or sin, with the qualifying expressions, "inward," "inbred," "original," etc. At the same time, I have no objection to the other terms, as long as they are used to mean the same thing, and not to tone down expressions until they have no point, nor to baptize evils under innocent names, in order to avoid the idea of a further cleansing from impurities or "inbred sin."

It is not my design to argue this question at length,

but to give a simple statement of how I was exercised on this subject, and how I arrived at the conclusion that it is proper to apply the term "sin" to those remains, qualified by "inbred," etc. There was a time when, to say the least, I doubted the propriety and correctness of applying the expression "sin," even in a qualified sense, to any remains of the carnal mind in the truly converted. I was cautious. I hesitated. I was, however, in search of light on this point. I had several conversations with an experienced minister, one who professed to be strongly in favor of holiness—who strenuously opposed the term "sin" in any sense as applicable to anything remaining in the converted. He admitted that there are remains from which the converted must be sanctified, but he had other terms than "sin" to designate them. At first I rather agreed with his views. But then he was so positive in rejecting all terms including the word "sin," and held so tenaciously to his views and his mode of expressing them, that it arrested my special attention. I was thus led to a closer examination of the subject. The fact was already admitted that there are remains from which we must be cleansed, and now the following questions presented themselves for solution:

1. What is the origin of these remains? 2. What is their nature? and 3. What is their tendency? This presented the question in its true light, and the answer came spontaneously:

First, these remains come from sin. All evil, whatever the degree, has its origin in sin. Secondly, they are of the nature of sin—the *remains* (the dregs?) (the roots?) of the carnal mind, of pride, of unbelief, etc., are of the same nature as the carnal mind itself, pride itself, and unbelief itself, are. Now, if the carnal mind, pride, unbelief, etc., are sin, which cannot be denied, is not that sin also which partakes of the same nature? Thirdly, their tendency is to actual sin; they lead to outward sin, cause the *committing* of sin. If these remains stir or move at all, it is to tempt to commit sin, or in concert with temptation to sin, in favor of sin, clamoring for indulgence in some act of sin. They are always on the side of sin.

The conclusion seemed inevitable. If these remains are caused by or come from sin, are of the nature of sin, lead to outward sin, they *are* sin, and it is proper to say so. Since *then* I have no hesitancy in calling them "inbred sin," etc.

All that I find necessary is, to be definite and specific in regard to what is intended by the term, and I see no danger in using the expression "inbred sin," etc. But is there not danger on the other hand? If we are so sensitive in regard to using the term "sin," however qualified, has it not the tendency to lead to the conclusion that these remains are rather innocent things, and that it is not of very great importance whether we be fully cleansed from them in order to serve the Lord acceptably, if they are only held in subjection, and that it is not essential to our salvation that we be saved from them? Is there no danger of pleading for Baal? These remains, by whatever name we may designate them, are not such innocent things that we can allow them without taking injury. We should never lose sight of the fact that they cannot enter heaven. We must be cleansed from them in order to see the Lord in peace. Let there be no trifling with them.

We may be thoroughly converted, and yet not perfectly cleansed from "inbred sin." If, however, we are sincere and faithful, the Lord will sooner or later discover unto us the need of a cleansing from the remains of the carnal mind, and thenceforth we must seek this cleansing in order to retain a fully justified state. If we know that we *are not*, and do not seek to *be* fully saved, we fall under condemnation. It must be our earnest desire to be saved from all sin, if we would progress in the divine life. At this point thousands falter. They feel their need of perfect cleansing, but they are not willing to make the necessary consecration, or for some cause, best known to themselves and their God, they fail to go forward and enter the Canaan of perfect rest, of complete salvation from "inbred sin." God does not countenance "inbred sin." He hates it with a perfect hatred, and has made provision for our deliverance from the same. It is the duty of every believer to seek perfect cleansing. Failing to do so is disobedience and brings guilt.

Reader, examine yourself whether you are in a fully-justified state. Examine your heart whether there are any remains of the carnal mind there. If so, are you earnestly striving after full salvation? Do not be discouraged, there is power in Jesus' blood to cleanse from every stain of sin. Claim the application of that blood, till you are made "whiter than snow." Believe that Jesus can, and will, and does save you now from every stain of pollution. Be saved to the uttermost. Why not, when this great salvation is within reach? There is *no need of any sin remaining in believers*. Praise the Lord! Jesus is "mighty to save," even from "inbred sin." Let every one that has this hope purify himself *"even as he is pure!"*

At this point I will also quote the following words from Bishop J. J. Esher on this subject. He says: "As true as it is, that the 'evil affections and desires' that still stir in the believer are not reckoned to him as sin, so long as they have not been discovered to him (*so lange er bei aller sonstigen Treue sie nicht erkennt*), so true it is also, that this remaining evil is reckoned to him as actual sin, as soon as it is revealed to him, unless he uses all diligence, according to the Word of God, to be delivered from it.

"But, at any rate, the actual existence of the 'evil' in the believer, whether known or unknown to him, is a disturbance of the order of God, that cannot well be branded with too strong a term. It is a superficiality, bordering on rank hypocrisy, to profess entire sanctification while all manner of selfishness is still cropping out; and how often this is done! So, also, to say the least of it, it is inadmissible to suppose that, although an evil principle, or generating power still remains in the believer, it is not sin as long as it is kept passive— *inactive*, and that it only becomes sin when it breaks forth into actual deeds. For, in the first place, a generating, or life power, cannot be strictly passive; then, again, the believer cannot keep it passive, without knowing of its existence, and its evil nature and effects, so that the matter of keeping this 'evil' passive, resolves itself simply into a conscious *cherishing* of an evil, and that is *sin*, actual sin.

"Poison is poison, though it be carried in golden cups; and to carry it, is high treason against God, whose likeness we must bear, in moral purity, through sanctification, by the blood of Christ. All evil,— call it principle, inclination, desire, lust, or a generating power,—is a disturbance of the order of God, and irreconcilable with perfect fellowship with God, through Christ.

"In entire sanctification all this is *radically destroyed*."

IMPORTANCE OF PERFECT PURITY

Under this heading Bro. Young continues his series by saying:—

More than simply development is necessary after conversion. The remains of sin are not removed by growth, but by cleansing. If we look at the nature of these remains, we must at once see the importance of a further *cleansing*. This does not consist in merely correcting habits, or changing the bent of the mind, but it is cleansing from all filthiness, an eradication of the roots of bitterness, or remains of the carnal mind; not a mere correcting of something which belongs there, and is only perverted, but the removal of something which does not belong there at all. Sin, even the remains of inbred sin, cannot be amended or corrected, but must be washed away; habits, bent of mind, bias of judgment may be corrected. Keeping these distinctions in view, will aid in arriving at the truth.

Great stress is laid, in the New Testament, on being cleansed from all sin, inwardly as well as outwardly, and on being made perfect, and presented blameless unto the coming of Jesus Christ our Lord. *Perfect* holiness is required.

But if perfect holiness is required to enter heaven, how is it with those who are converted and not wholly sanctified? Would they be lost should they die? Or have they holiness enough to enter heaven? Is conversion not a safe state? These questions might be answered by asking others, but that would not prove satisfactory. After much thought, we believe the following both Scriptural and logical, and hence tenable 1. That there are many who are truly converted and not wholly sanctified. 2. That none who are truly converted are lost, unless they backslide. 3. That no one, though truly converted, will be permitted to enter heaven without being wholly sanctified.

But if the truly converted are not lost, consequently are in a safe state as long as they remain justified, are they not also in a state fully qualified or prepared for heaven? Not necessarily. The truly penitent sinner cannot perish. He is, however, not qualified for heaven as soon as he becomes truly penitent. This is self-evident. He must continue to repent and believe till he is saved. If the true penitent, who is not yet justified, cannot perish, how much less the converted soul, who is not yet wholly sanctified! Both are in a safe state in which they cannot perish, but neither is in a state of being fully qualified for heaven. The converted person is much farther advanced than the penitent, but in both cases their remaining in a state of safety depends on their faithfulness in going forward. This is true of any state of grace. If the penitent should cease to repent of his sins before being pardoned, he would not only be still in an unsaved, but in an unsafe state. Even the converted, should they rest satisfied with their attainments, and think because they are in a safe state, they need no more, and should they neglect to go forward, to seek perfect purity of heart, would from that moment occupy dangerous ground, begin to retrograde, lose their state of safety, and backslide into dead formality if not into open sin. Many commit a sad mistake right here. They think they are the children of God and as such they cannot be lost, and conclude that if they only retain this state all will be well in the end whether they reach higher attainments or not; but before they are aware of it they have lost their first love and are retrograding. Believers becoming satisfied with a justified state, will make no efforts to be saved from the remains of inbred sin. If the assurance of justification is made the reason for not advancing to entire sanctification, this very assurance is thereby forfeited. This should stimulate the justified to shake off all lethargy, and consider that their continued justification includes the assurance of entire sanctification, and that it is the will and design, of God to perfect the work already begun. Christians should value their conversion, and the fact that they are converted should be a strong inducement to press forward to the glorious consummation of the work in perfect purity, and finally in glory.

The inquiry is sometimes raised, what becomes of those who die after they are converted, and before they are wholly sanctified? Sudden death, and deathbed conversions and many who lived exemplary lives, but who did not make a definite profession of holiness are cited, and the question is asked, how with them? We do not believe that any, who are truly converted and are faithful, *including the seeking of perfect purity*, die without being wholly sanctified. Not even if converted on a deathbed, nor in case of sudden death. This applies to the faithful. We are not speaking of the cold, or the lukewarm, but of those who are faithful in the performance of their duties, in seeking holiness and in all other matters.

Or take another view of the subject. Make two points, a starting point and an ultimate point. The starting point is conversion, the end heaven. Being converted you are an heir of heaven, and of all you need to qualify you to enter there, entire sanctification included. If you press on, if you are faithful, you will gain heaven, no doubt about it, but not before being wholly sanctified. The converted soul should consider the fact that he is a child of God, and that if faithful he cannot perish, of great importance, and should rejoice in it; but he should consider it of equal importance to be wholly sanctified, and should press on to it as an indispensable qualification for heaven. As certain as he is of gaining heaven if he proves faithful, so certain he is also of retrograding, backsliding and losing heaven if he is not faithful—seeking full salvation included.

But in laying so much stress on being wholly sanctified as a qualification for heaven, do we not sometimes too much overlook its importance in connection with our usefulness? To be useful in the highest degree we must be fully saved ourselves. A person who is truly converted may accomplish good, yea much good; but if he is fully saved he will accomplish more. One may do more good than another according to the gifts and talents allotted, but in all cases the more complete and full the consecration and cleansing, the more the heart is filled with the unction of the Holy Ghost, the holier and more earnest our zeal for God, the stronger our faith in God, the greater will be our usefulness. We know of ministers who preached the Gospel a number of years, leading many sinners to Jesus, who during this time preached entire holiness theoretically, without having experienced it, but did not succeed in leading any into its possession; but after experiencing it themselves, they were instrumental in leading others into the same experience. Then if you desire to be useful, as it is your duty to be, in the highest degree possible, be fully consecrated and devoted to God, be fully saved from all the remains of sin, be filled with the Holy Ghost and with the unction that abideth.

Perfect purity is of great importance because it is the will of God. "For this is the will of God, even your sanctification." We cannot be actuated by any higher motive to seek holiness than this, that it is the will of God. To please God should be our highest aim. It should be our meat and drink to do the will of our heavenly Father. Jesus teaches us to pray, "Thy will be done in earth, as it is in heaven." It is of the highest importance to our safety and happiness, that God be pleased with us. This he can be only when we render implicit obedience to his commands. We cannot obey him without seeking holiness of heart; for he says, "Be ye holy; for I am holy."

We should seek entire sanctification *now*. This is of great importance. Not next year, next month, next week or to-morrow, but *now*. If we do not seek to be wholly sanctified now, what do we seek? Do we not seek something less, just now, and so don't seek entire sanctification at all, as long as we pursue this course?

And can any one expect to reach it in this way? Not reasonably. The seeking must be brought to a point. We must desire and seek full salvation *now*, must, expect it *now*, must comply with the conditions *now*, and by faith appropriate the blood of Jesus, which cleanseth from all sin, *now*. Why should any wait, when all things are now ready? This deferring it to the indefinite future, is one of Satan's devices, which cannot be set aside too soon. We are quite certain that many would advance much more rapidly, if they would think less about with how little religion they may be safe, and more about the heights of salvation which it is their privilege to enjoy in this life.

"Gradual and Instantaneous"

The work of Sanctification is both gradual and instantaneous. The moment of perfect cleansing is reached gradually, but when reached the work is done in an instant. The approach to this instant may be like the approach to death, where life is slowly ebbing out till at last there is a sudden cessation of all the functions of life, and an instantaneous change is produced. Thus the process of the dying out of the "old man," whether it go forward rapidly or slowly, must at last reach an instant in which this carnal life ceases entirely. On this subject I again quote from Bro. Young.—

> He says: It is established beyond successful contradiction that the work of entire sanctification may be experienced instantaneously. Hundreds and thousands testify to this truth. We are not now speaking of the preparatory steps, but of the completion of the work. Cleansing from all sin may be experienced

to-day, *now*, if we make the proper consecration and exercise simple faith in the merits of Christ. In seeking holiness we should pursue the most advantageous and the safest course, and that is to obtain it as speedily as possible. We do not deem it proper to give any encouragement to anything that might retard the experience or work of holiness. We are, therefore, not strongly inclined to favor the gradual, in the commonly accepted sense of the term; but advocate the instantaneous. With all the arguments for the instantaneous, with all the importance of the work, and with all the inducements to seek full salvation *now*, the work, with only too many, is fully gradual enough, indeed some are gradually losing ground, instead of going forward. How would it be if the instantaneous work were not insisted upon at all? The stronger the instantaneous work is urged, the more earnestly perfect purity is sought as a present attainment, the more rapid will be the progress. Looking at it from the stand-point that the work is both instantaneous and gradual, we see nothing to lose and much to gain, by seeking entire sanctification now as an instantaneous work. Is it not our duty to make advancement in the divine life as rapidly as possible? And how can it be said that we are doing this if we seek holiness as a gradual work merely, when we may have a present, instantaneous experience of full salvation? It is God's will that we should be holy now. Glorious truth, that we may be saved from all sin now! We need not put it off. Even the young convert should seek it with all the power and energy of his whole being. The best way to keep from losing ground in religion, is to go on to perfection.

Should it be said, that some have experienced entire sanctification without being able to tell the hour or moment when the work was completed, it nevertheless remains true that there was a moment when it was done. In every work that is finished, there must be a moment of completion, whether it requires years, or days, or hours to reach that moment. This conclusion is unavoidable. And, there must be a moment when the consciousness is first realized that the work is wrought. This may also come, apparently, at least, by degrees, but there must be a moment when one is enabled for the first time to say: "I know that the blood of Jesus Christ his Son cleanseth me from all sin," and this is an eventful moment in the life of every believer who reaches this experience. In the most gradual process through which perfect purity is reached, the completion is instantaneous, and the completion really is the experience of the work. If we have experienced it, we shall know that the work is wrought, and have the evidence. A clear, definite experience is accompanied by a clear evidence. The experience and evidence may not in all cases be alike clear and definite, but all may know what is given them of God. All may, should, and if they properly examine themselves in the light of God *must* and *do* know whether they have separated themselves entirely from the world, have fully consecrated their all unto the Lord, and are relying upon, and implicitly trusting in the merits of Christ's blood to completely cleanse them, and whether the Spirit of God is gently and sweetly impressing the soul with a delightful and decisive persuasion that they are cleansed from all sin. These things may be realized by faith, so clearly that there is no need of being deceived. But it is a mistake to seek *the evidence* of holiness, instead of holiness itself.

Upon the whole the difference between the gradual and the instantaneous experience of entire sanctification seems to resolve into this: 1. The nature of the work is essentially the same in all cases, however much particulars in experience differ. 2. The general conditions upon which it is obtained are the same. All must come the same way, and upon the same terms. 3. When the conditions are complied with, God does the work without any delay. 4. Man's work—the preparatory steps—requires time; God's work— the cleansing act—is accomplished instantaneously, and is not measured by time. 5. Some reach the point of completion in a much shorter time than others. 6. Whether we reach the point when God saves fully, in five minutes or in so many years, the approach to it is gradual, and the completion instantaneous, and thus the work of sanctification is both gradual and instantaneous.

Let every one, then, resolve to seek and obtain holiness as speedily as possible. Let no time be lost. Retain all the ground gained and press on with vigor. God is ready to perform the work, why should *we* delay. Rush to the fountain of fulness, plunge in and be at once cleansed from all sin!

Purity and Maturity

We should, however, distinguish between purity and maturity. There is considerable perplexity in the minds of many by not distinguishing between them. Maturity always requires time, purity may be realized instantaneously. Maturity implies growth, purity is not reached by growth merely. Purity may be reached now, as in Wesley's time, within a few days after conversion. He says: "Many at Macclesfield believed that the blood of Christ had cleansed them from all sin. I spoke to them, forty in all, one by one. Some said they received the blessing *ten* days, some *seven*, some *four*, some *three* days after they had found peace with God, and two of them the next day." But were they mature Christians—fathers in Christ? "Maturity, or growth in grace, is, in an important sense, a question of time; purity is not. A free and full salvation from all sin is the present and constant privilege and duty of all believers. This will secure a rapid, solid, constant growth in grace. There is growth in grace both before and after the experience of entire sanctification." Rev. J. A. Wood says: "The process of CLEANSING AWAY and EXTIRPATING *sin* is one thing, and a *growth* or *maturity in grace* is quite another. These two things should not be jumbled or confounded. God never accomplishes that in the soul by *cleansing power* which it is the province of growth in grace to perform. On the other hand, a growth in grace *cannot* effect that which is the work of *creating, cleansing power*."

  The divine life and virtues implanted into the soul at conversion, need development. The believer must grow in grace and in the knowledge of Christ. The Christian character must be developed. Growth is indispensable at every stage of the Christian life and experience. There is growth before entire sanctification is experienced, as well as afterwards. Spiritual growth is illustrated by the growth of the body. There are babes in Christ, or little children, young men, and fathers. The child becomes a man by growth, or development. The same idea is taught by the figures taken from the vegetable kingdom. The fifteenth chapter of John furnishes a striking example. The main thought is the believer's union with Christ. The branch is united with the vine, and from it draws its nourishment, grows, flourishes, becomes fruitful. Growing, however, is not all, pruning is also necessary. Both ideas are here contained. Pruning is not growth, nor by growth, but by cutting; growing is not pruning, nor by pruning, but by receiving sap from the vine, and improving it.

  We should ever bear in mind that in regard to the believer who is not wholly sanctified, two things are necessary; namely, a cleansing from all filthiness of the flesh and spirit, and growth or development. The one is the removal of that which is not in conformity to holiness or purity, the other is the increase of the divine life in the soul, and the development of the Christian graces. Cleansing is by separation, throwing off, removing, washing away; growth is by adding, increasing, improving, strengthening.

The work of cleansing is to be completed before death, or how could we, after being "sanctified wholly," be *preserved blameless*, unto the coming of our Lord Jesus Christ. Indeed the figures used indicate the speedy destruction of the "old man," and removal of remaining impurities. Death by crucifixion does not require weeks, much less months or years. A thorough crucifixion insures a speedy death. Mortification is *speedy* destruction to life. The cutting off of a hand or foot, the plucking out of an eye, though extremely painful, are not prolonged operations. A few moments submission to the surgeon, and the work is done. So if we do our part in the work of self-crucifixion and mortification, God does his part speedily. It does not require great length of time to refine metals. The process of cleansing is generally quite limited. Sprinkling is a momentary act. Washing is soon performed. In every case the completion is instantaneous.

Not so with growth or development. This requires time. The child does not reach manhood, much less old age, in a moment. The acorn does not become the sturdy oak in a single day, or even year. Nor does it cease to grow when it arrives at a certain age. The child of God does not develop from a babe in Christ to a father in Israel at once; but in the use of the means of grace he is blest, receives new strength, and makes progress in the divine life. We are to "come in the unity of the faith, and of the knowledge of the Son of God, unto a perfect man, unto the measure of the stature of the fullness of Christ." We are not to remain babes, but to become young men, and fathers in Christ. Spiritual growth does not cease when we are wholly sanctified, but becomes more rapid than before. In development we see no attainment which admits of no further progress. Fathers in Christ still go forward, even to the end of their Christian career. New light is received, new strength is imparted, higher attainments are reached, greater fullness penetrates every avenue of our being; we are changed from glory to glory, and still the soul cries for new baptisms of the Holy Ghost and of fire; for more of God, and for still greater progress in the divine life. The soul drinks in more of the divine nature, and yet asks for enlargement both of vessel and of fulness. The path of the just shineth more and more unto the perfect day. *Complete cleansing* is what we must have, and anything short of it will not stand the test. Reach this experience as speedily as possible. It will not answer to weaken the "old man," he must be crucified, he must die. It is not sufficient to become purer, we become pure, "even as He is pure." To retain this purity, after it is experienced, we must continually go on to higher attainments.

Professing Holiness

It is a plain Scriptural duty to "tell what the Lord hath done for us." To Paul was this command given: "Thou shalt be his witness unto all men, of what thou hast seen and heard." Acts 22. 15. To this the Holy Ghost adds: (Acts 26. 16) "And of those things in the which I will appear unto thee." This points to Paul's *subsequent experience*. It was not only proper, but also a plain duty for Paul to tell the story of his conversion as he did on more than one occasion. In him we have a Scriptural example for professing our deliverance from the guilt and dominion of sin.

But Paul professes more than this. He claims an experience which includes the death of *self*; and this experience he professes thus: "I am crucified with Christ: nevertheless I live; yet not I, but Christ liveth in me; and the life which I now live in the flesh I live by the faith of the Son of God, who loved me, and gave himself for me." Gal. 2. 20. Here, again, we have a Scriptural example of profession, and it is such a profession as only those can make who are entirely sanctified. Whoever has experienced the crucifixion, the death, and the life, of which the apostle here speaks, need not be timid about following Paul's example in declaring the same. This, profession, however, is not made for the purpose of convincing others that we are pure, or holy, for if we are saved to the extent of perfect moral purity, the fact will be discovered by others even without our telling it. Just as others would notice our recovery from sickness, by seeing us again at our usual employment, so they will discover our purity by seeing the change that it has wrought in us. But then it would be an evidence of gratitude in us to speak of the physician and of the remedy through which we were restored. It would also prove a blessing to like sufferers with us, if we would recommend him through whom we had been made whole. In all this there would be no boasting, no egotism, but a praise of the good name of the physician, and a benefit to those who need his treatment. The application is evident. Gratitude to God prompts the wholly sanctified soul to tell the story of its complete emancipation. A desire to glorify God, and to see others enjoy a like salvation constrains the purified soul to "tell it all around." To suppress this gratitude, and this desire would be to neglect a plain duty, and to neglect a plain Christian duty is to suffer loss in our Christian experience— is a step away from the cross, and is likely to lead us still further away. It would seem proper then to profess holiness if we really enjoy it. But I do not contend for a stereotyped form of profession, much less for that harsh, egotistic mode of testifying into which some have fallen, whereby they are made to appear boastful and vain; but I would insist upon a fresh experience, from which there comes an overflow of humble acknowledgment of the things given us of God, in response to our consecration and faith. With such an experience we need not look either to the past or to the future for something to profess, for our life, our joy, our victory, our divine communion, are facts of *the present;* and, when these are humbly professed there is a convincing proof of the reality of the profession in the very expression of the countenance, as well as the tone of the voice. But there are other voices that must be heard on this subject. And here again I must quote from the editorial writings of Bro. Young. He says:—

> Having experienced entire sanctification, and received the evidence of it, should an open or public profession be made of it?
>
> This is a question upon which much has been said. Some are very conservative and cautious regarding the profession of holiness, seeing danger in urging a clear, distinct profession of a definite experience of the same. Others believe there is great danger in withholding the profession, when the work is experienced, and doubt whether holiness can be retained where it is not professed, citing numerous instances where the consciousness of full salvation was lost, because the testimony was withheld. It does appear that those who are clearest in their experience, have the least trouble about the profession, and as long as they give a clear testimony of having the experience, the Lord gives a clear evidence. No doubt some are in the mists, simply because they do not obey in testifying to the work wrought in their hearts. There are objections raised against professing entire sanctification, but as these generally come

from those who have no clear experience of full salvation, we, at this juncture, merely call their attention to the fact that to themselves a clear experience is of infinitely greater importance than endeavoring to settle questions which experience alone can clear up. Let us get at the truth in this matter, so that we may learn our privilege and duty, and come up to it.

A profession of religion is the acknowledged duty of all true Christians. This is generally recognized in the Protestant Church. Making such a profession is Scriptural. "Ye are my witnesses, saith the Lord." "Come and hear, all ye that fear God, and I will declare what he hath done for my soul." Jesus said to the healed Gadarene, "Go home to thy friends, and tell them how great things the Lord hath done for thee, and had compassion on thee. And he departed, and began to publish in Decapolis how great things Jesus had done for him. And all men did marvel." Jesus, immediately before his ascension, said unto his disciples, "But ye shall receive power, after that the Holy Ghost is come upon you: and ye shall be witnesses unto me both in Jerusalem, and in all Judea, and in Samaria, and unto the uttermost part of the earth." The apostles declared that they were witnesses for Jesus, and it is said they gave witness with great power. Paul declares, "If thou shalt confess with thy mouth the Lord Jesus, and shalt believe in thine heart that God hath raised him from the dead, thou shalt be saved. For with the heart man believeth unto righteousness and with the mouth confession is made unto salvation." To the Hebrews it was said, "Let us hold fast our profession." Timothy had "professed a good profession before many witnesses." Believing with the heart and confessing with the mouth stand, in the Scriptural sense, too closely connected to be separated.

And is it not the duty of those who make a profession

of religion to tell the whole truth? Should not he who undertakes to relate his experience, as a witness for Jesus, tell *all* that he has wrought in the soul? The more Jesus has done for us, the more we are able to relate to his glory. Are we justified freely? Then we can tell the wonderful story that we are adopted into the family of God, are sons of God, and joint-heirs with Christ Jesus our Lord. Glorious truth! Children, and therefore heirs of God! Do we realize that we are *fully* saved; and should we not also tell this to the glory of God? Can it be said that we truly and property confess Christ without acknowledging the whole truth? Jesus desires faithful witnesses. Does he authorize us to conceal any part of his gracious work in our hearts? Is there no danger of denying our Saviour by keeping back part of the truth? But says one, "Profess it with your life." Is this sufficient? We know that a life of holiness is essential to give weight to the profession, but at the same time the confession is to be made "with the mouth," unto salvation. We cannot conceive why it is not just as much a duty to profess holiness as conversion, by those who have experienced it. As a general rule what is applicable to the one is also to the other. We fully believe this, that if any one experiences holiness, and the Holy Spirit prompts him to make an open profession of it, he cannot refuse without taking injury to himself. The Spirit of God will teach us in these things, and we cannot disobey without grieving Him. The fact is, when the heart is full of holiness, holy fire and zeal, it will have utterance, and the testimony will be given with a holy boldness, and humble trust in God, and an unction which those who shrink from a public profession, yet desire to be considered *wholly* sanctified, can neither gainsay nor successfully imitate, should they attempt it. To shrink from professing holiness, or to profess in equivocal expressions, in order to avoid the responsibility, or in any way get around it, is wrong, and persons doing so cannot retain sanctification, nor can they *obtain* it, if this is their principle before they are sanctified. There must be no shrinking here. We must frame no excuses for the purpose of getting around the cross. Christ needs, can use, and will own none who are ashamed of him, his work, or his cause.

As a general thing profession should be made. It is a blessing to those who do so. It commits them for holiness, which is just as it should be, but which many wish to avoid, and, on this rock, of non-committal, they make shipwreck. Profession cuts off retreat. We should cut clown the bridges, make no provision for retreat, but cross the Rubicon, pass on, and maintain the ground we have gained by pressing on to higher attainments. Profession shows that we trust that he who has cleansed is able to keep clean. It is a means of overcoming the devil. "And they overcame him by the blood of the Lamb and by the word of their testimony." It is a blessing to others. Those enjoying holiness are refreshed, and receive new courage to go on, when others testify to this great grace. Seekers after purity of heart are led to see the way more clearly and desire the blessing more eagerly. The indifferent are waked up, and are brought to see that there is something lacking, and many resolve to seek holiness, when they hear others profess it. Sinners are moved, melted and led to Jesus. Eternity alone can tell the good that has been, is, and may be done by professing a present, full and free salvation. The work of holiness, and the work of the Lord generally, flourish better where it is professed by a humble testimony as well as an exemplary life.

Is it not extremely inconsistent to teach, that man must be saved from all sin, must be wholly sanctified in this life, and that it is the privilege and duty of every child of God to be fully saved, and then turn round and caution in regard to professing it, as though it were the hardest thing in the world to reach this experience and live consistently, or, as though there were a mystery hanging around the profession of it which was very difficult to solve? Is it consistent to set up the standard of full salvation, and then discourage the profession of it? Does this not discourage the seekers and hinder the experience?

We love to see men and women full of the Holy Ghost, committed for holiness, standing up boldly for Jesus, and laboring for the cause. Oh, how the Lord does bless such! He meets with his witnesses, and when they testify, he gives *"showers of blessings."* The Holy Spirit fills them, and Pentecostal baptisms fire up the soul in holy love to God and man.

Then, ye who have experienced full salvation, humbly, but boldly profess Christ as your complete Saviour. Think of the good you may do. Improve every opportunity. Soon your lips will be sealed in death, and you will no more be able to tell your friends and neighbors of this great salvation. Tell them of it while you may. Lead to Jesus as many as you can. Go on then, experience, exemplify, spread and profess full salvation, till the aliens of darkness shall be put to flight, the gates of hell tremble, sinners fear and quake, and cold professors grow pale on account of the power of God manifested in the sanctification of believers and the salvation of sinners. We need more holiness in experience, profession and life. We need more witnesses of full salvation, more holy men and women, who are pointed, definite and radical in the work of holiness; who from experience, with a glowing heart, will testify of its fulness continually. The Lord continue to raise up hosts of faithful, living, burning, shining witnesses: of the truth that "Jesus *now saves to the* UTTERMOST!"

Again he writes: It seems to me there is too much squeamishness in regard to professing holiness. There has been so much criticising, toning down, modifying, and objecting, that one might almost be led to think criticism was the great holiness panacea. All the defects of the holiness work are brought to bear against professing holiness. Of course if the professing were out of the way none could be criticised as a professor of holiness. That would silence the clamoring, but it would at the same time dispose of the entire holiness idea. Silence the testimony, and you may as well write, "*Ichabod.*"

I need not tell you how this squeamishness originated, how it was fostered, how it developed, the fact is before us. I am afraid the blame does not all rest with the opposer. The tendency of some friendly cautions and criticisms has been to *dis*-courage rather than to *en*-courage the profession of holiness.

I have thought already that too much attention is given to the professing of holiness, by objecting to, and modifying expressions, endeavoring to bring everything within the sphere of a certain line of phraseology, and not enough to the bottom-work of a holiness experience. When any blunder is made, or any conduct manifests itself in one professing holiness, which is not consistent with his profession, the professing is at once assailed and the idea advanced, that we should be very careful, and that such a one should make no such profession. True, the life should correspond with the profession. But is there not another, a better way of solving this question? Why not drive in a different direction? Why not direct such to the blood of cleansing, urging them to bring up their experience to their profession?

The idea of professing holiness, as I understand it, is not to *convince* people that you are sanctified, but to glorify God and edify your fellow-beings, by telling what the Lord has done for you. We can, as true witnesses, only testify of that which we have experienced, and are expected to tell the whole truth. The experience is what we need first, and then the testimony. We need thoroughness in experience, and liberty in professing. If your heart is full, you need not hesitate to give your humble testimony.

Now, if the experience is the main thing, why be constantly working at, mending and modifying the profession? Why not rather encourage believers and say to them: "Seek full salvation! Rush to the fountain of cleansing and be washed! Look by faith to Jesus, come fully under the blood and be made whiter than snow! Be baptized with the Holy Ghost and with fire! Follow the Spirit-do not run ahead—follow the Spirit, as he leads you in testifying for the Master. Assert your liberty! "Should the language in professing holiness not meet with the approval of the fastidious, never mind, if the heart is right and filled, a little blundering in language will not do very much harm.

If the attention could be turned from this cavilling in regard to professing holiness, and directed to the promotion of the experience, we would soon see an end of this squeamishness. If the efforts that are made to tone down the professing of holiness, were made to raise the experience to the true standard, and encourage the work, what results might be achieved!

Let all get under the blood, and abide there. Let all become "wholly sanctified," keep brimful of perfect love, and be guided by the Holy Ghost, then professing will take care of itself.

In 1870 Rev. R. Yeakel wrote some words of instruction and caution to "Professors of Entire Sanctification," in which he says:

"1. Be sure that you do not profess entire sanctification unless you *know* that you possess it. 2. But if your experience is genuine and Scriptural, and the Holy Spirit assures you of the 'things given,' which will soon begin to be confirmed by corresponding fruits in your life—do not hesitate to confess Jesus *at once* as your *perfect Saviour*, and recommend him as such to other believers. This is your sacred duty, and is a condition of your continuous future salvation. Only those that *use* the 'talents' entrusted will increase and be found worthy in the end. Christ will confess only those before his heavenly Father and his holy angels who are not ashamed to *confess him before men*."

Two Kinds of Profession

In 1873 the same writer published his experience in a series of articles, in the *Living Epistle*, at the close of which he points out two kinds of profession. This distinction he gives clearly and correctly in the following words: I was regarded as a professor of "holiness" or "sanctification" on our circuit, though I had never made any profession in such terms. Having learned the depth and exceeding loathsomeness of my depraved "self," which I knew well enough had all been washed out by the blood of Christ, and the holy Saviour filling me with the Divine nature, yet I felt a strong repugnance to using the personal pronoun *I* in telling of it. I could not bring myself to the use of phrases like these: "*I am* entirely sanctified;" *I am* holy;" for Scripturally and truly speaking, it was "*not I* but *Christ in me*." He had become the moral center, the second Adam, *substituting* the first Adam within me.

This led me to search the Scriptures on the subject of the "profession of holiness." To my surprise I could not find anything whatever of it in the Bible, when the subject of *confession* was under consideration. On the contrary, I found commands directly and indirectly enjoining the confession of the PERSONAL CHRIST *as our Saviour*. I read what Christ said: "He that confesseth ME before men, him will I confess before my heavenly Father and the holy angels." Here I found a mutual, personal confession taught. When I read of Christ, that he is "made unto us of God, wisdom, righteousness, sanctification, and redemption," that according as it is written, "He that glorieth, *let him glory in the Lord*." I saw that Christ is both our sanctification and the subject of confession, and all the good we have, and all we have to say about it is *"in the Lord,"* who dwells in us by faith. Again, when I read, "Wherefore, holy brethren, partakers of the heavenly calling, consider the Apostle and High-Priest of our profession (*'whom we confess,'* according to some other translations). Christ Jesus," I saw again that CHRIST personally and officially is the subject of confession. I need not multiply quotations, as the New Testament is full of it in unequivocal terms. This confession, however, is not to be made in an Antinomian sense, glorying in Christ with the lips, while we live in sin, but in the Scriptural sense of *"Christ being formed within us* the hope of glory," thus cleansing, sanctifying, saving, and using us for his glory.

Entire sanctification considered as a definite experience is Scriptural, but to make IT a subject of confession is not Scriptural, and will do nobody any good. The glorious *Blesser* is to be confessed and exalted in all his work, but not the blessing. It will not do to talk of the blessing *chiefly*, and call that confessing Christ. The Bible enjoins, throughout, a direct, personal confession of Christ, in explicit terms. We must put him always in the front, exhibit him in word and life; our goodness as well as our badness must be left behind, and nothing be seen and known, but "Jesus alone" — and Jesus *"all* and *in all."*

I could then say: *"Jesus saves me fully; his blood cleanseth me from all sin; he is my sanctification; he sanctifies me wholly, and keeps me*; and thus confess *him* in his work, and give him all the glory, but I could never say: *"I* am saved; *I* am pure; *I* am holy; *I* need not keep the blessing of holiness, *it* keeps me;" leaving out Christ and speaking of *"I"* and *"it."* The latter idea that *"it* keeps me," is altogether groundless, the blessing cannot and does not keep itself nor anybody; Christ alone saves and keeps us now and evermore. To him be all the glory!"

"The Holy Ones"

This significant title is the German form of the phrase "The Saints," by which term the true people of God are distinguished from unbelievers. Being a term employed by the Holy Ghost, in the inspired writings, it is evidently well chosen, and properly applied to the class which it is intended to designate. Blessed are they who rightfully bear the honors of this title! It is more significant than all human titles put together, and yet it may be conferred upon a child, or upon persons who are illiterate, or poor. It belongs to all the children of our Great King.

It is no dishonor to any person, in whatever position he may be, to be classed with the saints. If he is holy in the sense that God requires us to be holy, he can even afford to be persecuted for "belonging to the holy ones."

Concerning this subject Bishop T. Bowman wrote as follows, for the *Epistle* of 1878:

> This term, which occurs nearly a hundred times in the Scriptures, and seems really to have been a favorite term with the inspired writers when speaking of those who have become partakers of the Divine nature, has been used by many who profess to believe the Gospel, only to express contempt for those to whom they ap-

ply it; just as if the endeavor to become holy were itself proof of sanctimonious hypocrisy, and as though all earnest godliness on the part of men was but hollow pretence, And this is done, too, in the face of the explicit declarations of the law of heaven, that only the pure in heart shall see God, and that without holiness no man shall see the Lord.

That such things should be met with in denominations which are composed principally of men and women who are dead in trespasses and sins, and strangers to the covenant of Israel, living without God and without hope in the world, relying for future salvation either on their Church-membership or the sacraments; and the corner-stone of whose doctrine seems to be, that we are all miserable sinners and must remain such until we die, is not strange. That they should raise the cry of fanaticism, and sound the note of warning against being over-zealous, and that they should exhort to a daily confession of sin and be over-anxious lest some earnest ones might speak with a little too much enthusiasm about that which the Lord has done for their souls, is rather to be expected; for nothing is so destructive to their business of selling souls for naught than downright earnest holiness, which has no communion with the unfruitful works of darkness, and which sings of God's mercies and talks of his mighty love, and his wondrous grace, and witnesses of his power to save even to the uttermost, and rejoices with joy unspeakable and full of glory, in the possession of that perfect peace which passeth understanding. Its beauty charms, its power convicts, and its logic is irresistible.

But why some men in our own Church, which has given the doctrine of holiness such prominence, at whose altars every minister has either declared in the presence of God and the people that he is in possession of entire sanctification, or has solemnly obligated himself earnestly to seek this state of grace—why these should be under the necessity of continually defending their orthodoxy, and should feel themselves called to stand upon the watchtower and sound the note of alarm whenever and wherever efforts are made to advance on the line of holiness, seems strange. Here and there, it is true, some have run into dangerous extremes; in a few congregations extreme measures have been made the standard of orthodoxy, and now and then some one has used extravagant language; but while these things have been, and, I presume, will continue to be of occasional occurrence, hundreds, yea thousands, are bringing reproach upon the Church, are perplexing the weak and distressing the strong, are full of envy and ill-will, and pride and covetousness, resting content with their condition, because, forsooth, under a certain kind of preaching, in which conscience and the demands of the Bible to be holy and undefiled are very lightly touched, their minds become somewhat excited, and, under a certain kind of singing, their sensational and emotional natures get somewhat aroused, and they have had "a good time," although they have no victory over sin, no real peace of mind, and no willingness to make any sacrifice for Christ.

And yet how seldom do we hear from the lips of these over-cautious, conservative men any earnest, stirring, whole-souled appeal to the lagging ones to come up to the front, to take more advanced ground, to give themselves wholly and without mental reservation to Him who died for them. Why are these things so? Do we not find the answer in the fact that our doctrine on entire sanctification is not fully believed and accepted? Either it is held that we are made entirely holy in the hour of conversion, so that there remains neither impurity of the flesh nor of the spirit, and no need for further and deeper purification by the blood and the Spirit, or else that there is doubt whether we can be saved from all sin before death, and hence it becomes his, instead of witnessing to the power of the blood to cleanse from all sin, " to lie in the dust every day and cry, God be merciful to me a sinner."

O dear brethren, in view of the many sickly ones, the many that sleep, and the many who, I fear, are dying spiritually, let us lift high the standard of the cross! Let us cry aloud, Behold the Lamb, whose blood presents us holy, without spot, or wrinkle, or any such thing. While we ought fearlessly to check extravagance, the trumpet ought to give no uncertain sound. Place no "ifs" or "buts" in any of your sermons or exhortations as to the ability and the willingness of our Redeemer, who is Lord of all, to save unto the uttermost, and to present us without blemish before God, if we give ourselves into his hands wholly and unconditionally, and trust him fully. O Lord, revive thy work! Amen!—

After reading these pointed words from the Bishop, the reader will doubtless be interested in hearing his voice further. Hence, I next quote from one of his sermons. The theme of which is

Going on to Perfection

His text is Heb. 6. 1, 2, on which he speaks thus: I presume it will be necessary for me to define what we are to understand by the term perfection. It should not be necessary for me to say that neither absolute nor angelic, nor Adamic perfection can be meant.

These, it must be conceded, are impossibilities, and Paul was too sober a man to exhort his Christian brethren to run after an ideal to which it was impossible to attain.

1. It is not perfection in knowledge. This would imply infallibility. As there is often knowledge without grace,

so frequently there are great depths of grace with a very limited knowledge. Sin may be expelled, but much ignorance remain, although divine knowledge combined with love greatly promotes true holiness, giving the mind clearer comprehensions of duty, and more delicate views of God's holy will. Upon the other hand holiness increases our knowledge of divine things, hence the Scriptures combine growing in grace with knowledge, still at least in this life our knowledge cannot become perfect.

2. It does not imply freedom from temptation. This is evident from the fact that although our first parents were created in righteousness and true holiness, yet they were liable to temptation; and our Saviour who knew no sin was tempted in all points like as we are—tempted to forsake his mission for worldly honor, to be selfish, to act presumptuous, yea, even to worship the devil! Hence, we shall always be liable to temptation. However, it is no sin to be tempted; it is only a sin when we yield to temptation. Only when temptation hath conceived doth it bring forth sin.

3. It does not imply the extinction of our animal propensities. These are a part of our nature, inherent and essential to our constitution. Adam certainly possessed them in Paradise. The Saviour of the world had them. The Bible nowhere condemns our propensities as sinful. Their gratification in forbidden objects, or in an inordinate degree offends God and enslaves man. It is, therefore, not the province of religion to destroy them, but to regulate and control them, and render even the lowest instincts of our nature, faculties by which to glorify God.

4. It does not imply exemption from the danger of falling away. Certainty it diminishes that danger, because we are farther removed from the tempter's influence, and live nearer to God, yet as we remain in

a state of probation while on earth we cannot be beyond the reach of danger. The exact doctrine of our Church on this point is thus formulated: "Sin has, as it were, lost all its power against such an one, he being surrounded by the love of God as with a wall of fire. The flesh, the world, and Satan are under his feet, and he rules over his enemies; yet watching, and not slumbering."

5. Nor does this state imply incessant rapture. Freedom from slavish fear, peace—perfect peace, is promised, and thank God, may be enjoyed, but tears and anxiety and sorrows will remain while on earth. We find Elijah in grief, and Jeremiah in tears, and Paul sorrowful, although he rejoices. Even our Saviour wept— wept because Lazarus was dead; he also wept over Jerusalem. In this valley of bitter disappointments the holiest perhaps find more cause for sorrow and tears than they find occasions for rejoicing. Still, thank God, there may be and is inward peace while bitter tears may be coursing down our cheeks.

Having shown in what this state does not consist, I proceed to speak positively as to what Perfection does imply. First, however, allow me to say that it must mean something—that this term would not be used so frequently in the Scriptures if there were no meaning attached to it. Allow me to quote some of the more prominent passages of the New Testament in which it occurs: Matt. 5. 48; 2 Cor. 13. 11; Heb. 13. 20, 21; 1 Pet. 5. 10; 2 Cor. 13. 9; Col. 1. 28. Now certainly these passages, these exhortations and promises must mean something. It is more than simply an empty term.

1. It implies perfect control of our animal propensities, or as they are sometimes termed, our natural passions. It is certainly true that in a limited sense every child of God has control over himself, does not walk after the flesh, nor fulfil the desires of the flesh and of

the mind, but has been delivered by grace. However, it is a matter of universal experience, according to both the Bible and our Book of Discipline, that young or weak Christians, sometimes yield more or less, either voluntarily or negligently. The perfect Christian, however, stands so firmly and immovably that he can parry and gain the victory over any temptation the moment it may present itself. Hence it is complete victory over our propensities and passions. "The flesh, the world, and Satan are under his feet, and he rules over his enemies; yet watching and not slumbering."

2. It implies deliverance from all evil affections and desires. Not, as some have indicated, an extinction of desire. This, would be equivalent to, an extinction of being — of existence; but deliverance from desire for gratification in evil, from love for that which is forbidden, and inclination towards that which is opposed to right. That usually the regenerated are conscious of desire for and inclination toward sinful gratification is a fact which it is useless to deny. They restrain these desires, however, because they know it is wrong to indulge them, and because it leads to ruin, and displeases God. Christian Perfection implies that our affections and desires lean towards the right, that sin in all its varied forms, and in its most attractive features, becomes repugnant, and holiness is desired and loved for its own sake. To do God's will becomes the passion of the soul, and is its meat and drink. Hence, the perfect Christian bears no ill-will against any human being, and will not in any manner avenge a wrong, but he has a loving forgiving disposition. Charity hides a multitude of sins, and what it cannot hide it will forgive.

3. It implies perfect resignation to the will of God, so that we follow whithersoever he leadeth, through good

and evil report, poor or rich, in sickness and in health, through honor or dishonor, in prosperity or adversity, even giving thanks unto God the Father in all things. When love has become perfect it casts out all tormenting fear, and cries: "The Lord is my shepherd, I shall not want." —

Entire Sanctification

Here is another editorial voice which gives distinct utterance on holiness, in the *Christliche Botschafter* of 1877. It is the voice of Rev. M. Lauer, the Senior Agent of the Evangelical Publishing House.

He says: It is a cheering fact that Protestant Christendom is comprehending more and more the glorious truth, that it is the duty as well as the privilege of all true Christians to be cleansed from all sin, i. e., to become wholly sanctified by faith in Jesus Christ. Sanctification has its beginning in the new birth. Every regenerated person is, by virtue of his regeneration, also sanctified, but not wholly sanctified. He is not sanctified throughout soul, body, and spirit. He who has been born again, has indeed become a new creature, but is not yet wholly sanctified. At the time of his justification the sinner obtains full pardon, and with the new birth he receives the power with which he is to have dominion over all sin; still he is not fully cleansed from all filthiness of the flesh and spirit. By virtue of his regeneration he is a child of God, and is called to a holy walk, a fully consecrated heart and life, perfect cleansing, and an inheritance with the saints in light. But notwithstanding this high calling, the experience of the regenerated testifies that there is still something that is sinful, cleaving to them inwardly, which often becomes a burden, and at times is the cause of severe conflicts.

Most of those who remain faithful and endeavor to serve God uprightly, after they have been born again, soon become conscious of the fact that there is still something remaining which is inclined to pride, anger, self-exaltation, wilfulness, selfishness, etc. I do not assert that the experience of all regenerated persons, concerning the points alluded to, are alike in proportion. With some it may be only one or two sinful affections which seek to assert themselves. With others, they may also differ in their power. But all feel, almost daily, that there is still something remaining from which they must be saved, i.e., fully sanctified.

Now here comes the important point to decide. Shall we teach that the child of God must continue in a state of such besetments; or that it is sufficient to simply keep these sins in subjection? Can the gracious state of regeneration be at all maintained by virtue of such consolations? I doubt it. Is it not much better and safer to show to all who have the beginning of the inward Christian life, the full plan of salvation according to the Scriptures, namely, that they may, through faith in Jesus, be saved from all sin, be cleansed even from the last remains of sin, whether it be in the spirit or the will,—yea, that they may be wholly sanctified through faith in Jesus? Most certainly. The Lord desires to restore his full image in all his children. Whoever becomes indifferent about striving for entire sanctification, after he is born again, "indulges in fleshly lusts which war against the soul" (1 Pet. 2. 11), allows the "old man" to reign (Rom. 6. 5-11), grieves the Holy Spirit, and will certainly make shipwreck of faith (1 Tim. 1. 19). As justification and regeneration must succeed genuine evangelical repentance, so also in experimental religion entire sanctification is required after regeneration, for "without holiness no man shall see the Lord" (Heb. 12. 14).

Our salvation through Christ is complete. He is willing and able to save us wholly from all sin; yea, even from inherited depravity, and to sanctify us "through and through." I believe that in the experience of every converted person a period arrives when, unless he earnestly seeks entire sanctification, or has already experienced it, he cannot well make any progress in true godliness. Several of the most eminent Protestant divines of different denominations hold this view. Drs. Dorner, Stier, Julius Mueller, Rothe, and others assert that it is in the very nature of things, that without the earnest seeking or possession of true holiness no abiding blessing of God can follow. Paul, in writing to the Hebrews, says: "Now the God of peace, that brought again from the dead our Lord Jesus Christ, that great Shepherd of the sheep, through the blood of the everlasting covenant, make you perfect in every good work to do his will, working in you that which is well-pleasing in his sight, through Jesus Christ; to whom be glory forever and ever. Amen." (Heb. 13. 20, 21.) Every Christian is inwardly to love, perfectly, that which God loves, and hate that which he hates, and thus, to a certain degree., become like God. To this end, entire cleansing from all sinful affections, entire sanctification, is requisite, "because it is written, Be ye holy; for I am holy. (1 Pet. 1. 16.) This sanctification Jesus will accomplish in the hearts of all his children who earnestly desire it by the cleansing power of the Holy Ghost, through faith in him, and on the ground of his accomplished atonement. By entire sanctification they are to be made holy.

I here give the substance of the testimony of several other noted theologians regarding this doctrine. Watson says: "Sanctification includes our entire deliverance from all filthiness of the spirit as well from inward depravity, as also from filthiness of the flesh arising from the sinful use of our senses and the members of our body; also the impartation of the love of God so fully in us, that our hearts are wholly subdued by it." Archbishop Leighton writes concerning entire sanctification: "As our spirits and bodies in the power of Satan formerly resisted God, to the same degree they now render willing obedience; not a part, but the whole commandment is comprehended in this love; man is not partially, but wholly, not for a time, but forever, subjected to him." Bishop Foster says in his book, entitled "Christian Purity, or the Heritage of Faith," substantially this: "We believe that it is the privilege of every Christian to attain to a state of grace in which he is, in the proper sense, entirely free from inward and outward sin, a state in which he will not do anything wrong, in which no unholy desire is in him, in which the whole outer being of life and the whole inner being of the heart is pure before God—not according to his absolutely perfect law, but according to the law of his Gospel which he has given unto us." To the definition given by Wesley of *heart purity* and *salvation from all sin*, inward and outward, the whole Methodist Church subscribes. In the symbols of the Reformed Church there is a direct reference to sanctification. So we find in the Swiss confession of faith, in the article concerning the Church, that the same consists of the congregation of the saints, and which, as the bride of Christ, through whose blood she has been purified, shall finally be presented to the Father without spot.

In our book of Discipline, under the Article on Christian Perfection, it is asserted that our Church, too, holds to the doctrine of entire sanctification and Christian perfection. Our membership should frequently and attentively read this Article. In it the main point, that sanctification consists in being fully saved from all sin—that is to say, from all evil affections and desires—is established.

Concerning the doctrine of sanctification and Christian

perfection, the Evangelical Association does not wish to be misunderstood. The General Conference of 1867 advised our ministers most earnestly to use such expressions and modes of speech, both in their private teaching and in their public ministrations, in regard to this highly important subject, as not to be misunderstood, nor lead to departures from the plainly expressed sense of our doctrine, so that there be one opinion among us, and, as near as possible, the same mode of expression be used.

No theory and no argument should be enunciated by our preachers, in word or writing, which is in conflict with our doctrine of entire sanctification or Christian perfection. Our Church holds it to be in accordance with the Scriptures. We have taught and believed it from the beginning. The practical part might be emphasized more, and, in general, be more thoroughly experienced and practiced.

NO HEAVEN WITHOUT HOLINESS

Under the title "A Ruinous Error," I find the following in the *Epistle* of 1869, from the pen of Rev. H. B. Hartzler, the present editor of the *Ev. Messenger*. He says:

> The sinner sometimes thinks and says that God is too good to banish any soul of man from his presence and the glory of his power forever. Professed Christians oftentimes think, if they do not say it, that the Lord is too gracious and kind to exclude them from heaven, even though they are consciously remiss in duty, and deliberately divide their services between God and Mammon. Some say that if one is a good Christian (?) in all other respects, a merciful God will not banish him from the presence of his glory merely because of a lack of holiness.
>
> But how strangely do such characters misapprehend the goodness of God! How direct the antagonism between such views and the teachings of the Bible! *God is*

too good to receive an unholy soul into heaven! It is his *goodness* that forever will and forever *must* exclude the impure and unholy from his heavenly kingdom, and from the purity and glory of his presence. We can see what sin is in its nature and tendencies. We can read it in the tears, and woes, and groans, and sorrows, and blood, and graves of our world, and in the lurid light of a quenchless hell.

Shall God keep no spot in the vast universe untouched by the hellish defiler—no place where those who love and possess holiness, and hate and avoid sin, may dwell forever, secure from its approach, in an atmosphere of untainted purity? Could God be good if he would open heaven, with its blood-washed, holy millions, its radiant spotless angels and archangels, and receive sinners who passed by the fountain of blood unwashed, refusing to become meet for his holy kingdom?

No! no! God is too good to blast the hopes of all the good, the pure, the holy. Do you see what would come of it if the unholy should be permitted to enter heaven? Look at it, and then tell us whether God *could* be good if he would welcome unholiness there!

The sinner, unsaved from his sins must be as wretched in heaven as in hell. Sin in heaven would be sin still—an infectious, devilish, tormenting disease that would blast, and blight, and ruin whatever it touched. The unholy, then, would gain nothing by being admitted there, while the holy would sustain infinite loss. What possible motive, then, could exist, or what reason could be found for taking the unholy into the celestial city?

Beware how you venture your soul on a hair-bridge across the bottomless abyss! Without holiness no man shall see the Lord! God *cannot* give the unholy a place with himself, while he is good and gracious, holy, true, and just. And will Jehovah deny himself and abdicate his throne to give you heaven because you will not wash in the cleansing fountain of the Redeemer's blood? O stupendous folly of a dying worm! Go, tremble before Infinite Purity, bow your will to the requirements of his word, and "be ye holy," for He who calls you is holy!

Our Sanctification Personal

Another voice of no uncertain sound, which was frequently heard through the first volumes of the *Living Epistle*, is that of Rev. S. L. Wiest, the present Corresponding Secretary of our Missionary Society. Concerning our personal sanctification, he says:

> If we keep to the old land-marks we shall always be safe; but the moment we get beyond, we are in danger. We find a great many sincere defenders of holiness allowing themselves to be drawn away from Bible language and Bible sense, in order to make the experience of sanctification less obnoxious to opponents. They make concessions which seriously invalidate the grand fact that *we* are sanctified through the atonement of Jesus Christ. They, to a certain extent, separate believers from their sanctification. This is as erroneous as to separate our sanctification from Jesus Christ.
>
> The idea has found currency that as Christ is our sanctification, he covers our deformities, and we may retain our inward depravity and be saved from sin, and its consequences. This, we think, arises from the great stress, that is laid upon the expression, "Christ is our sanctification." That Christ is the author and source of our sanctification admits of no question, but he is this to every believer, whether he is sanctified wholly or not. Christ suffered and died in our stead, but he cannot be holy in our stead. Although Christ is the sole meritorious cause of our sanctification, yet, unless we

through him become purified, even as he is pure, we have not yet made a *personal appropriation* of him as our entire sanctification. We may believe that Christ is our sanctification, and fail to realize the transforming influence of this great work in our hearts, because we may misunderstand the full intent of Christ as our sanctification. However, we cannot fail to realize in our lives the blessed results of holiness when we believe that Christ *sanctifies us*. Our sanctification is not to be a covering unto us, but it is to be *a part* of our nature. We are to be thoroughly imbued, throughout our entire being, with holiness. Christ prays for his disciples, "Sanctify *them* through thy truth; thy word is truth."

Here is a personal application of sanctifying power. The Bible teaches that *we* are to be sanctified wholly; that *we* are to be made perfect in love; that *we* are to be made pure; that *we* are to have clean hearts; that *we* are to be cleansed from all filthiness of the flesh and spirit; that *we* are to be holy; because God is holy. It is Christ's design to destroy—root out—all the deformities of our moral nature. When the work is fully accomplished then *we* are wholly sanctified; yet, at the same time, inseparably connected with the author of our sanctification.

The sanctifying power of the Holy Spirit is not only to complete the work, but it is to remain with us forever.

We are never to be without it. We must retain it constantly, or we fail. It is our property, as all other things are, in Christ Jesus.

Concerning the time

When We may be Sanctified,

Bro. W. says: The *fact* that the Bible teaches a difference in time, in our regeneration and entire sanctification, is so evident that it has been received as an established truth in theology. The following passages will make it plain to all candid inquirers: "And I, brethren, could not speak unto you as unto spiritual, but as unto carnal, even as unto babes in Christ. *For ye are yet carnal*; for whereas there is among you envying, and strife, and divisions, are ye not carnal and walk as men?" Having, therefore, these promises, dearly beloved, let us cleanse ourselves from all filthiness of the flesh and spirit, *perfecting holiness* in the fear of God. "For this is the will of God, even your sanctification." "And the very God of peace *sanctify* you *wholly*." "Sanctify them through thy truth; thy word is truth."

These Scriptures all refer to *believers* who are not wholly sanctified. Although we do not deny that there may be cases where persons are wholly sanctified in conversion, yet we believe such cases are rare. Experience unites with the Bible in teaching that the entire sanctification of the believer is a work wrought after regeneration.

If then, believers are sanctified but in part when converted, how soon may a consummation of the work be expected? The Scriptures have fixed no time, but they say to all men, saints and sinners, "Now is the accepted time."

The Conditions of Our Entire Sanctification

Is not a certain preparation necessary before the believer can enter into this blessed state? Undoubtedly there is. The sinner, before he can be "born again," must comply with certain conditions; and so the believer must make certain preparations, or comply with certain conditions, before he can be wholly sanctified. This preparation is hastened, and the glad moment approaches in proportion to the *earnestness* with which the believer pants for a *clean heart*. There is no period in the history of any true Christian when he has not a personal interest in the work of entire sanctification. Babes in Christ are urged to "go on to perfection." It is our *privilege* and *duty* to seek after perfect love as soon as we are members of Christ's kingdom. God is no respecter of persons, but rewards all who diligently seek him. We would, therefore, say to every inquirer, "now" is the time to seek entire sanctification; "now is the day of salvation."

HOLINESS A BIBLE DOCTRINE

Hark! another voice has spoken! It comes from the East, where wisdom and true orthodoxy are supposed to reign. As far as I know no one ever questioned either the ability or the theological soundness of this familiar evangelical voice. I refer to Rev. Jesse Yeakel. In an article in the second volume of the *Evangelical Magazine* he discusses the subject of Bible holiness thus:

> Concerning this highly important subject, to which the attention of so many is unusually drawn at present, there are *three* facts which are so evident, that they cannot escape the notice of any unprejudiced Bible reader.
>
> FIRST FACT:—*The Holy Scriptures recognize all regenerate souls as being sanctified, and therefore call them saints*—Read: Rom. 12. 13; 1 Cor. 1. 2. and 6. 11; Eph. 5. 3; Col. 3. 12. So also the believers of Lydda (Acts 9. 32), of Jerusalem (Rom. 15. 26), of Ephesus (Eph. 1. 1), and of Philippi (Phil. 1. 1), were called "saints."
>
> This well-established Bible doctrine finds sufficient proof in this:
>
> 1. That every regenerate soul has obtained the pardon of all sin, through faith in Jesus Christ. This needs no further proof.
>
> 2. That every regenerate soul is delivered from the

dominion of sin. Whoever has not obtained victory over sin, is still a servant of sins and, consequently, is not born again. Herein is established the saying of Paul, that where sin did abound, there grace did much more abound; because he that is regenerated has victory over sin. Read Rom. 6. 14-22; Col. 1. 13; 1 John 3. 6-10. Admitting that not many who obtain grace, walk according to this standard, yet this does not change the matter, for the cause is not *in the grace*, but in *our yielding*. This circumstance cannot change the Bible standard of regeneration.

3. That every soul that is regenerated is walking in a new life. This is a natural result of the facts already stated, and the proof of it is so well established in the daily life of such, that further evidence would be superfluous. Read Rom. 13. 12; Eph. 2. 3; 1 Pet. 1. 14 and 4. 3, 4.

SECOND FACT. *The Scriptures teach a further cleansing of believers, and hence, the holiness that is begun in them is not perfect.* Read Mal. 3. 3; John 15. 2 and 17. 17; Rom. 12. 1, 2; 2 Cor. 7. 1; Eph. 4. 22-24; Col. 3. 9, 10; 1 Thess. 5. 23; 1 Pet. 2. 1, 2; 1 John 3. 3; Heb. 12. 14.

Besides the absurdity of the thought that in the life of a "babe" in Christ, in which holiness is a feature, there should already be a perfection, let us also consider the following facts, which confirm the above passages of Scripture:

1. The difference that is often manifest between them and the pattern of holiness set before them in the character of Christ. It need not be argued here that we must have the mind that was also in Christ; that we are to follow him in his footsteps. But it might be well for us to take special notice of a few of these footsteps. First of all, let it be remembered that *during all his earthly life it was the chief aim of Christ to do the will of his Father in heaven.* Although

in possession of the greatest wealth, the highest honors, and the most perfect happiness: he submitted to the greatest poverty, the deepest humiliation, and the severest sufferings. More: He gave *"himself."* The last and most exalted of these footsteps is this: *"I delight to do thy will"* — even if it lead from riches to poverty, from honor to humiliation, from happiness to suffering, *yet* I *delight* in it! — And now, beloved children of God (I don't mean the lukewarm or the backslidden), how about the *"following"*? You have experienced the new birth; but were then all ungodly self-seeking and striving after worldly honor, ease and comfort, so totally destroyed, or rooted out of your heart, that you could always heartily repeat the language of your great exemplar: — "I delight to do thy will, God"? Can you imitate your Divine Pattern in this, even if it lead you into poverty, scorn, and suffering? Oh, how positively facts testify to the contrary!

2. This fact is further confirmed by the voice of conscience, from all sincere children of God, of all times. But of this inner voice little would be known if it had not given expression in almost innumerable writings, songs, and confessions. Who has not already heard the many lamentations and deep sighs of such, because of their injurious weights and besetments? Who has not heard the fervent prayers of these earnest souls for deliverance from these evils? Verily, we cannot mistake these voices! And — mark you, the voices do not come from those who have grown cold in love, not from the dead members of the Church, not from the backsliders; but from the upright, earnest, faithful ones.

THIRD FACT. *The Holy Scriptures teach that there is a perfection of holiness — a state of being sanctified wholly, or through and through.* In Matt. 5. 44-48; Eph. 1. 4 and 1 Pet. 1. 15, 16, *our entire sanctification is set forth as being the will of God*, as plainly as words can tell it. In Eph. 5. 27; Tit. 2. 14 and 1 John 1. 7-9, the same is set forth just as unequivocally as the *end for which Christ gave himself*. A few passages which speak of our (subjectively) *becoming such*, and of the manner of attaining to it, deserve more particular notice here.

The prophet (Mal. 3. 3) speaks figuratively of the purifying of silver and gold; and who does not know that the result of this is entire purification? According to Matt. 3. 33, the three measures of meal which receive the leaven become *entirely* "leavened." In Rom. 6. 11, we are taught to be like Christ, by *being dead indeed unto sin*. In 1 Cor. 7. 1, Paul exhorts us to *perfect purity*. According to Eph. 4. 22 and Col. 3. 9, the believers are to *put off* the old man, and on the other hand, they are to *put on* Christ.

They are to be *renewed* in the spirit of their mind,—they are to *put on* the new man. (Eph. 4. 23, 24; Col. 3. 10.)

These passages and figures, which we hear expressed every day, are so clear, so expressive, so appropriate, that we need simply to let them mean what they say, not only to know the truth, but also to speak in perfect harmony with our previous quotations, concerning the will of God, and the end for which Christ gave himself—namely for our sanctification. Let us consider further:

1. That faith in the *divinity* of Jesus Christ, whom we acknowledge as our model, demands that we recognize the ability of his mediation as *sufficient* for us, in order that we may be enabled to walk in his footsteps, i. e., to live holy as he is holy. To deny this latter, would, according to all reason, be incompatible with faith in his divinity.

2. That faith in the divinity of the Holy Ghost, who is acknowledged to be one with the Father and with the Son, demands that the sanctifying efficacy of the same

be considered adequate to our sanctification, as God the Father wills it, and as God the Son has provided it. To deny this, would, according to all reason, be incompatible with faith in the divinity of the Holy Ghost; yea, with faith in a divine trinity.

Whatever objections and questions human criticism may offer concerning the doctrine of holiness, there is a solution, according to the rules of criticism; and, even if there were not, these are less than nothing in comparison with the distinct utterances of the Divine Word; for when the Lord speaketh all the earth should keep silent. Meanwhile the most important matter is, that we *become* and *be* what the Divine *"thou shalt"* demands. Be sure of this, that to the Divine *"shall"* is also joined a corresponding *can;* for the commands of God can never stand opposed to his promises.

THE "HOLINESS MOVEMENT"

The attention given by some of our writers to the so-called holiness movement deserves mention at this place. Even *friendly* criticisms, which point out errors and mistakes, while at the same time they give words of encouragement to help the "movement" forward, are voices that should be heard. But *the good fruits* of this wonderful revival of holiness, with all the defects that may accompany it, must not be overlooked. Indeed they must be apparent to all unbiased readers and observers. The first voice on this subject is from Rev. R. Yeakel, Principal of Union Biblical Institute, at Naperville, Ill. He writes thus of

ITS DEFECTS

I have always considered the holiness movement as a work of God, because of its unselfish commencement, and the spirituality and earnestness of its first leaders, who certainty did not enter upon this work to seek place and high salary, much less the applause of men or the friendship of carnal professors and the world, but aimed right for the heart, and preached the Word of God with divine unction and searching power. And the measures they adopted were in the main appropriate, and adapted to bring men to the "valley of decision" for God and his cause. I attended but one National Camp-meeting—some years ago—but the power of God that prevailed and penetrated the thousands present, so that sinners in many cases could not resist it, and believers also were carried forward into the unfathomable love of God, convinced me then and there that *God was in the work*, and that it had a mission to accomplish in the Church. And this conviction has not been shaken in the least by all the unfair criticisms and many spiteful remarks and insinuations of some religious papers. If such writers could see what a sorry little figure they make in using the magnifying glass of prejudice and hatred to turn little blemishes that unavoidably cling to even good men and means, into great mountains, they would quit such small business, and turn their weapons upon the devil's kingdom, where there are castles and fortresses of darkness enough to demolish!

By no means would I hereby say that this movement needs no advice or even correction. It does; and I often have wished more of it would be given *in the right spirit*. It has its faults and weaknesses, and if some of them are not cured, it will end in failure. I will name a few of these.

1. In my humble opinion its greatest lack is, that it pays too little attention to a *thorough discovery of remaining moral depravity in believers*. It is true, theoretically, this is postulated, but how seldom do the

writers and preachers of entire sanctification searchingly dwell upon it, and show the necessity of first knowing deeply and even painfully the *need* of such sanctification. And yet a deep knowledge and urgent realization that the believer *needs* to "perfect holiness," lie indispensably at the bottom of true sanctification. If one does not realize the need of it, he can never exercise faith in Christ for it, and he never will. We must first be hungry and thirsty, in order to eat and drink; we must first realize our disorders before we apply to the physician for cure. Without this, conversion will be superficial, and the same holds good on psychological and theological grounds, with reference to entire sanctification. Nearly all superficiality and self-deception are directly attributable to this deficiency.

2. Again, in my opinion, there is too little of *outward* sanctification preached. Too much dependence is placed upon the assertion that the outward will take care of itself, provided the *inner work is right*. According to the Bible both must be practiced together, and we find that the apostles wrote and preached a great deal on the outward appearance and conduct of believers, and insisted that they should *lay off* outward acts and things that were not pure, and even flee the very appearance of evil. The Word of God and true holiness enter into and purify *all departments of outward life and practice*, as well as the inner man...

I have a deep conviction that the "movement," with all its untold good, lacks in these and several other respects. As to other points, that "enemies of holiness" — and I use this expression deliberately — endeavor to make as to certain eccentricities and personal peculiarities of some who are specialty engaged in this movement, they are not worthy of notice. And such stigmas as "Inskipism," and

"*Inskipwesen*" as one sneeringly called this movement, will do as little harm as "Abolitionism," "Wesleyanism," etc., did in their day.

As far as my observation goes, this movement has been conducted somewhat too much upon the line of certain measures and methods *in some sections*. I have not a word to say against the use of sensible and appropriate measures to bring men to decisive action at certain crises in religious progress. The "mourner's bench," or, as we now call it, "altar work," has always been such a means among us and the Methodists—and our Evangelical fathers very frequently also used special means to promote entire sanctification as a distinct work and experience, such as raising hands, coming forward for prayers, standing up, etc. The blessed Saviour himself did at times request those who wanted to be healed to do special things.

But when means and measures become *stereotyped* or a mere *habit* they lose their appropriateness and usefulness, and when they are relied upon and in whole or in part substituted for the searching proclamation of the Word of God, and the convincing and cleansing power of the Holy Ghost, then they become positively detrimental to the work. I am afraid too much of this has been mixed with the "holiness movement." And yet withal I have no doubt that it was well meant, though not wisely used.

This leads me to another point. In its later years this movement has been to a considerable extent guided and controlled by young, inexperienced persons. When I say *young* I mean such as have been recently converted, or, perhaps, been reclaimed from a lukewarm condition. A writer in the *Christian Standard and Home Journal*, endorsed by the editor, Rev. J. S. Inskip, makes the following points in this direction, which say precisely what I wish to say: "It is lamentably true that some unworthy, a good many irresponsible, and many warm-hearted, zealous, but unqualified persons have pushed themselves out as evangelical workers. They are unqualified for two reasons: First, they have but just been converted, and have usually come into the experience of holiness at the same meeting. In from three to six months thereafter they have pushed out into evangelistic work. Secondly, many of them are quite young and very impulsive. In their zeal they are a little inclined to denounce pretty freely all who call in question their call to, or fitness for work. They sometimes denounce the Church," etc. These remarks doubtless apply more particularly to things occurring within the M.E. Church, but may not be quite amiss among us. To my mind the main fault with such young "holiness leaders" is their idea, that they were converted *and entirely sanctified at the same meeting*! I doubt not they had some such impression, received, perhaps, from what they heard from others around them. From all I ever could learn from experience, observation, and the Bible, the idea of conversion this hour and the *next hour* entire sanctification, *without knowing the nature, need or distinctness* of entire sanctification—is a delusive impression. And being started this way such persons are apt to go by impressions. The writer above quoted says further: "They think they are led exclusively and unerringly by the Holy Spirit, deal largely in impressions, and somewhat in dreams and visions. Those who fall in with them become like them," etc. The "holiness movement" can only suffer by such well-meaning, but deceived persons. It ought to be led by experienced and scripturally wise men, who are full of faith and the Holy Ghost, and able to discern and judge from having their spiritual senses well exercised. *These men*, especially those who are placed at the head of the

Church, ought to *take the lead,* and by preaching, writing, leading and adopting proper measures, awaken the Church and *keep her wide awake on this glorious doctrine* and experience, striving *mightily in the power of God to present every believer perfect in Christ Jesus.*

I had already commenced to write on the *bright side* of the "holiness movement," when I deeply felt the necessity of touching a few more of its defects, for they seem too serious to be overlooked in this connection.

1. There is a slight deviation in doctrine, from the straight line of the Scriptures, and also of our article on Christian Perfection, by some of the teachers, and a few of the leaders in this movement. I here refer to the assertion frequently made, that sanctification is in no sense gradual; that it is not attained under a process of growth in grace; that all spiritual advancement between regeneration and entire sanctification has *no* cleansing effect, but is *preparatory only* to an instantaneous cleansing thereafter. This view has obtained a standing from the fact that there exists an opposite extreme view, viz., that there is no such thing as an entire and instantaneous sanctification; that there is only a growth in grace. And, as a matter of fact, this growth is, in many cases, no growth at all, but a lukewarm, worldly-minded, world-conformed state of Christian profession. This latter is a fearfully prevailing fact in the Churches with which the holiness movement battles. Now, in combatting an error, the opposite truth must be stated strongly, and in such conflict it has often been the case that some have leaned to even the opposite extreme. So here.

Rev. J. A. Wood, for instance, in his very excellent book, "Perfect Love"—which thousands have read with great benefit—goes so far as to define growth in grace from this extreme stand-point, as being "the improvement of the present stock of grace in the heart" (p. 61);

which would, of course, be no growth in "grace" at all, but a growth in *graces*, viz., the practical improvement or application of the grace received by faith in our Lord Jesus Christ. I could never find in Scripture that a believer has at any time "a *stock* of grace" in possession. Saving grace is received by faith from Christ, moment by moment, as we need it. The parable of the vine and the branches illustrates this point definitely. Christ is the vine, we are the branches. "Abide in me and I in you," says He, "then ye shall bring forth much fruit." "Without me ye can do nothing." "If a man abide not in me he is cast forth as a branch, *and is withered*" As in nature, so in the kingdom of grace there is *never a stock on hand* in the branch: it receives sap continually from the vine; and, hence, as soon as the connection is interrupted it *begins to wither and die*. Again, take Paul's illustration of the head and the body, or the members. The member must *continually receive* blood and life or it will fail, it has no *stock on hand*.

One among the many test passages on this point is Ephesians 2. 8: "For by grace are ye saved through faith." It is evidently the grace of our Lord Jesus Christ that *saves*, as received by faith. From what does it save? From *sin*, as we see from the connection in this chapter. Now, Peter connects growth in grace and the knowledge of our Lord Jesus Christ together (2 Peter 3. 18). Every true Christian knows that true knowledge of ourselves and of Christ are vital elements of faith, and that the increase of *such* knowledge also increases faith, which results in the reception of a larger measure of grace; and a larger measure of grace has again its blessed reflex influence upon knowledge and faith. They go together and involve each other, and their progress is called *"growth"* in the Scriptures, and it is such in its very nature. And in *this* growth there is a *gradual* salvation from inbred sin just as fast as sin is discovered, faith exercised, and saving grace received, for grace saves—it cannot be otherwise. And this is the way in which the Holy Ghost leads a number of true Christians, yea, some of the very best ones. Our article on "Entire Sanctification" in the Discipline calls this growth a *"gradual change"* and says that the state of Christian Perfection is "ordinarily attained gradually by an upright course of life in following the Lamb," and that, "however, this work is perfected in the soul, sooner or later, by a sudden and powerful influence of grace and outpouring of the Divine Spirit." Here, then, we have a gradual sanctification ("change"), perfected by an instantaneous completion of the work. This gradual change is in its rapidity conditioned upon the faithful following of the Lamb—as he leads by the Word and the Spirit—the more the Word is searched and the Spirit obeyed, the sooner the work of salvation from all sin will be completed instantaneously. This is the true principle and doctrine as so beautifully formulated in one of Mr. Wesley's conferences: "When faith begins, then holiness begins, *as faith increases, holiness increases*, when faith becomes perfect, holiness is perfect." The reader will see by this time that I do no harm to instantaneous sanctification, but give to growth in grace that which is scripturally and theologically its due. And this is the true plane upon which the holiness movement ought to move.

2. Again, I ought to mention another defect, viz., the *counting* of those who are said to have been sanctified at a meeting, and *publishing this number* in the papers as being *reliably* correct. I find nothing at all in the New Testament of such counts. Conversions, it is true, have been reported by exact number in the Acts of the Apostles. But, then, conversion is a much more *outwardly* marked transition, and it was especially so in the days of the apostles. But in our day, even, this is

seldom reliable, as there are, alas! not a few "revivals" made by arrangement, according to order, almost without repentance and prayer, and much less outward change from refined popular sins to righteousness.

Professions of entire sanctification there may be as many as are reported, but how many of them know really what they are speaking about; how many of them have had a proper knowledge of the need of full salvation, and a hungering and thirsting to realize the all-cleansing power of Jesus' blood, as had Jacob Albright, George Miller, John Dreisbach, J. B. Taylor, William Carvosso, Hester A. Rogers, Bishop Hamline and thousands of others whose experience was accordingly deep, durable and reliable? How many were perhaps only revived from a lukewarm state? How many carried along simply by the general stream of blessed influence? As things go rather superficially *in our days*—by "rapid transit" at times,—I can't help feeling misgivings when I read positive statements that *so many hundreds have been sanctified* in such and such a short time, and consequent conclusions drawn that the work of holiness is *"progressing wonderfully."* I know that the Holy Spirit can and will work powerfully and quickly, when and where he is sought as suitably and earnestly as did the One Hundred and Twenty, until the day of Pentecost came, with its overwhelming showers; but where there has been no such realizing of need, and no such earnestness, I feel like placing an interrogation point after these reports. Will not the holiness movement by counting too much and too fast, run out into *shallow water*?

The Bright Side

The first ray of this "movement," that now shines upon my mind, is the general and emphatic revival of the doctrine that entire sanctification—in its negative aspect—is an *"instantaneous"* work in contradistinction from an imperceptible gradualism in religion, which is said to be completed only in, if not by death. Such gradualism has proved itself practically, almost without exception, to be that "lukewarmness," which is so exceedingly distasteful to the Holy One of Israel (Rev. 3: 15,-16). It is at the same time usually conformity to and compromise with the world.—There is "death in that pot!"—I have, however, wished sometimes that the word *"distinct"* would be used instead of *instantaneous;* it would better express the exact truth of the work, for this experience never takes place literally in an *instant* —an indivisible point of time or a moment—it is often progressing an hour, a day, even a week until it becomes clearly accomplished. It is true, faith which takes Christ for our sanctification, as he is made unto us of God, lays hold upon him as such in an instant, all things being equal, but the receiving, and adjusting (if you permit this word), and the clear assurance of this full indwelling, i.e. the *experience*, takes more time than an instant; it is, however, a *distinct process* in consciousness. Now this fulness and distinctness is also held up in our Church Discipline as a glorious object and aim to be set before believers as very desirable, and as a great inducement and means to a rapid growth in grace, thus hastening speedily the experience of the distinct work, whereas, on the contrary, stagnation takes place.—The "holiness movement" is doing a good and much needed work in "insisting" upon this point, if only the proper and real gradual work is not overlooked, as our Discipline so well and wisely combines both. An aimless, indistinct sanctification is not taught in the Bible, but there is a "perfecting" (*completing* in the original) of holiness, a becoming "sanctified wholly," a cleansing "from all sin," being made "white in the blood of the Lamb," most clearly and emphatically taught, prayed for, and insisted upon in the Holy Scriptures. Thanks be unto God that this is being held up and insisted upon strongly and powerfully. The Holy Ghost will sanction and seal such doctrine as the truth of God!

Another bright ray is the fact that *regeneration* as the work of the Holy Spirit is insisted upon as a prerequisite to holiness. As far as my personal acquaintance goes, sounder conversions have taken place in connection with the work of holiness, than in some highly-extolled revivals gotten up by appointment.

Again, it is a praiseworthy feature of this "movement" that it attacks especially certain features of conformity to the world, such as parties, Church fairs, sociables etc., etc., gotten up for carnal pleasure, and money-getting for church purposes, by pandering to the wishes of the world and unconverted members of the Church. (Alas! that there are such in the Church.) These are works of the devil, nicely fixed up, and learnedly excused; and in not a few places the work of soul-saving must sometimes be stopped for the time being, to give place to polite and refined soul-destroying, by these fleshly inventions. I am glad that the "holiness movement" wars against them. We bid it God-speed, and send our best wishes and prayers along!

Furthermore, there are some scintillations of light visible in the attacks upon the nearly all-prevailing sin of conformity to the world in the matter of "pride of life," especially in fashionable dress, about which most preachers and writers of our day are as silent as death—or if they must, perchance, speak of it, it is done in the softest way possible. However, it would be only good if the "movement" would speak oftener and louder on this subject—for many, *many* in the Church are exchanging their souls for a few bits of gilded tin and tinsel, and disposing of their Saviour for a few gewgaws made of silk and cotton!—Many worship the goddess of fashion most devoutly in the house of God, and the cock in the pulpit does not even dare to crow at this practical denial of the blessed Saviour!—Against some other popular sins its trumpet gives a clear sound which is very reassuring.—"Cry aloud and spare not;" it is greatly needed.

Another ray of light is the earnestness, fervent prayer and spiritual aggressiveness that characterizes the "movement." These are excellent features. The Holy Spirit does certainly cooperate with those who with one accord earnestly call upon the name of the Lord. As far as I am acquainted with the "movement," I would specially refer by this remark to the National Holiness Association—they are men of much earnest and fervent prayer. And I am glad to know that nearly if not quite everywhere they insist upon the Biblical, Methodistic, Evangelical and appropriate mode of *kneeling before God* in prayer!

In connection with this point I ought to mention that *fasting* on special occasions—a practice recognized and recommended in our Discipline, as well as in the Bible—is duly respected in the "movement," and is another item to its credit.

It deserves very favorable mention, likewise, that the grand truth comprised in the word *"consecration"* —a living sacrifice to God—the devotement of spirit, soul and body to the Most High and his service, for time and eternity, is emphatically taught and, as I verily believe largely practiced.

On the bright side of this movement I reckon also that very thing which some have considered its chief fault, viz., the adoption and use of public decisive measures, such as standing up, raising the right hand, kneeling down, silent prayer, etc. True the *abuse* and the *stereotyped use* of such measures is harmful, as I showed when writing on the other side of this subject; but a proper and judicious use is good, and especially adapted to get men out of old worn-out "ruts" into decisive action Our Saviour ofttimes adopted certain measures for a wise end. The man with the withered hand was required to "stand forth" in public meeting, and there stretch out his withered hand before all the people, and upon complying with the request he was healed. The blind man was ordered to go to the pool of Siloam and wash, and as he went and did so, his sight was given him. Lepers were directed to go and show themselves to the priests, and as they obediently went they were cleansed, etc.

Christ often healed without any measures, but also very frequently with them. So he often works still. Very many sinners have been pardoned and believers sanctified by the immediate application through the Holy Spirit, of Scripture passages, like: "Behold the Lamb of God that taketh away the sin of the world;" or, "The blood of Jesus Christ his Son cleanseth us from all sin." Often, also, while standing up by request, and publicly repeating these or similar words, by which action faith was helped into a lively and decisive exercise, salvation has been received. The fathers of the Evangelical Association did, long before the present "movement" commenced, use special measures with seekers of entire sanctification, such as standing up raising the right hand, kneeling at the altar, etc., and it very ill becomes a minister of our Church to condemn the proper use of them.

One of the very best measures ushered into quite general use, may here be recommended, viz., the expressing or relating of spiritual experience by the adoption and repetition of Scripture texts, and stanzas of spiritual hymns, by which useless verbiage, irrelevancy, and unedifying stereotyped sayings, are avoided. By "telling experience" in this manner, faith is strengthened, and both conviction and edification spread among hearers. The use of the Word of God, especially from believers' hearts and mouths, is always accompanied with the unction of the Holy Ghost, the blessed Inspirer of the Word.

Another very good thing must be noted in this connection, which is the plain, unadorned preaching of the Word of God, aiming directly at the heart of the hearer. Oh, that this only true method of preaching might be re-adopted by all who have deviated from it!

Allow me to dwell finally upon one other important point. I refer to the great improvement in the manner of holding and conducting camp-meetings. When the second National Camp-meeting was held by the National Holiness Association, at Manheim, Pa., Rev. R. Dubs, then Editor of the *Christliche Botschafter*, employed the now sainted Rev. S. G. Rhoads, as correspondent, to describe the meeting in said paper. Bro. Rhoads gave a description in detail, of the arrangements of the encampment, of the order and manner of public worship and religious exercises, of the pointed and powerful preaching, of the marked results, etc., etc., which placed the meeting before our Church like a panorama. About that time there was a growing feeling in some parts of our Church that camp-meetings had accomplished their mission, because in many cases the spirit of picnics began to make inroads upon these meetings, and the leaders did not see how they could prevent it. The meeting at Manheim showed the way. They commenced the day with an early prayer meeting, and from that time on continued the work almost without intermission until ten o'clock in the evening, changing about successively with prayer, confession, seeking salvation, testifying, preaching, exhorting, secret prayer, holding children's meetings, and other special gatherings, etc., giving no time for lounging and loafing, making everything pointed, definite, and stirring towards the great end in view, viz., salvation through the blood of the Lamb. This had a thrilling effect. Other reports from subsequent meetings intensified it, and the result was a great improvement in holding and conducting camp-meetings throughout the Evangelical Association, and beyond her borders.

And now, in conclusion, I pray God to reinvigorate this movement by the powerful operation of the Holy Spirit, and lead it still more in this direction, that Christ may be all and in all, and every believer be made perfect in him!

Among the many leading preachers of the Church, who have stood up in defence of *special* meetings for the promotion of holiness, no one has spoken in stronger terms than Rev. S. L. Wiest, whose prolific pen greatly aided the spread of holiness during the earlier part of the present "movement." Writing in defense of "holiness meetings," he says:

There have been objections raised against meetings held for the *special* object of promoting holiness. Some seem to regard them as of no use, and some look upon them as a source of division and strife.

1. To the latter class I would say that strife and divisions never originate in "holiness meetings," hence they should not be discontinued on that account. If Satan and evil-disposed persons object to them, it is only an evidence that good is being accomplished through them. They are no eyesore to men who love the Lord Jesus in truth. It is only worldly-minded and coldhearted professors who are afraid that men may get too much of the Spirit of Christ.

2. Is it right to hold meetings of this nature? *Are* they of any use? I believe it not only right, but emphatically

necessary. I do not think that all who are not Christians should be excluded from such meetings, because they often result in the conviction and conversion of sinners. The same spirit that sanctifies also justifies.

Among believers in the doctrine of holiness it is admitted that Christians ought to attain to this state of grace as soon as possible after conversion. To gain this point they need instruction and encouragement, apart from sermons, etc. The duty and privilege of being *wholly sanctified* must be kept constantly before the minds of the people, or they will become indifferent.

"Holiness meetings" answer this purpose better than any other means. It is true, Christians may seek holiness at home, but they find themselves in the same position a sinner does who endeavors to seek pardon at home. A public committal for holiness is a sure step toward it.

Experience teaches that ten believers are sanctified wholly in " holiness meetings" to one at home. This alone is sufficient to establish their propriety and utility. Moreover, the proper help and sympathy are always found in these meetings, for such as seek this blessing, as well as for those who need advice and encouragement in the way.

In 1879 Bishop K. Dubs wrote as follows concerning this "movement":

I may be pardoned for making a few remarks in reference to the so-called "holiness movement," which was, at least in certain circles, more urged and pushed a few years ago than at the present time. I do not wish to be understood as though our ministers had not urged holiness of heart and life before this latter so-called "special holiness movement" became so prominent before the Churches. Our ministers preached earnest self-denial, complete consecration to God, the crucifixion of the flesh and the lusts thereof, a complete, radical separation from the world, in all its forms and customs, purity of heart and life; in short, a full and entire deliverance from all sin, and a life fully devoted to God, and yet I could but rejoice that this doctrine of entire sanctification, which is certainly the central idea of experimental Christianity and the crowning doctrine of our faith, was so strongly presented to the believers, and the attainment of that state of grace so pressingly urged upon the attention of the Church. All this was in accordance with our belief and in the direction of the spiritual completion of the individual disciple and the Church as a whole.

It must be evident to every close observer that the intensity of that "movement" has materially decreased, so much so, that I felt it my duty to endeavor to arouse even some of the former and most prominent advocates of this cause. I am not ignorant of what has caused, at least in part, this "calm." Injudicious leaders endeavored to enforce measures and methods which produced harm, and the dissonance " between the profession and the life of others caused not a few Christians to hesitate and refuse to follow the directions given. But I know also of men and women who adorn this profession with a holy life. We may become too cautious, too conservative, too critical, too sober; hence I would say to all my brethren, Let us emphasize with all diligence, and enforce with all possible directness and unction, a free and full salvation, attainable by all believers in our Lord Jesus Christ. We can avoid the extravagances, and urge the work, in all soberness of the Gospel, with a heart aglow with the power of the blood of the Crucified One. Worldliness is pressing hard upon the Church, indifference about a faithful discharge of our religious duties reigns in not a few hearts; more, far more perish on account of this than being too zealous and too earnest in the service of the Divine Master.

During the same year Bishop Thos. Bowman wrote on the same line after this manner: I find it much easier to detect errors and point out defects than to suggest a more excellent way. Usually, there is much apathy in regard to the experience of entire sanctification, which has quite properly been termed "the central experience of Christianity." There is a lack of plain, earnest preaching upon the subject, and at many places the services are simply a round of pleasant entertainments without any object in view. The prize of our high calling in Christ Jesus is not held up before the people as it should be, and there is but little real striving after entire heart purity. Even the truth taught so prominently in the Bible and our Discipline, that it is the privilege of every believer, long before he dies, to attain unto this 'central experience of Christianity,' if not openly questioned, is nevertheless considerably below par, and its advocates are, more or less, to express it mildly, opposed.

> It is sad, indeed, that so many connected with the holiness movement, have led injudiciously, and have frequently, and that quite needlessly, provoked opposition. It is as useless as it is impossible to deny these facts. They are too prominent, and too well known.
> However, ought not some of us who have not been recognized leaders in the movement, who have stood aloof — although in full accord with the doctrine to which our Church is so fully committed, namely, that entire heart purity is attainable in this life — because we found it impossible to endorse all the measures adopted, come forward and stir up the Church from centre to circumference to make renewed efforts to attain unto this "central experience"? While some have taken a step backward, re-

alizing, probably, that they had been a little "wild," might not we, with perfect safety, take a step forward, and, profiting by their mistakes, fling to the breeze the banner of full salvation more strongly, more clearly, more definitely than ever, and call upon the people to go up with us and possess the land? Many of our people will soon die, and it is evident, as is known to many of our ministers and to each one of our Bishops, that they do not enjoy complete victory over sin, and are not saved from all evil affections and desires. May not their blood be upon us? Lord, send forth thy light and thy salvation!

THE VOICE OF THE BISHOPS IN 1879

It is the experience of the Evangelical Association, as well as of other Churches, that the days of her greatest prosperity were those in which she gave the most attention to holiness.

This fact is supported by the testimony of the entire board of Bishops, as expressed in their Episcopal address to the General Conference at Chicago in 1879. The following paragraph is a quotation from the address to which I allude:

> "There is nothing to hinder us from drawing freely from the great fountain of truth, the revealed will of God, the Holy Scriptures; nor is there any conceivable motive that should influence us to forsake the 'form of sound words.' All our interests bind us to the plain, untrammeled Word of God. This marked freedom of belief, together with the conviction, grounded upon a living faith, and confirmed by the Holy Spirit, that we abide in the truth, should move us to guard with exceeding watchfulness against all superficiality in teaching or experience, or any departure from the pure and divinely attested doctrines of our Church, especially

the doctrine of full salvation from all sin through faith in the Lord Jesus Christ—from its condemnation and power, in justification and regeneration, and from its pollution in entire sanctification, all accomplished by the Holy Ghost, who dwells in us to confirm this doctrine, and to clearly assure us of our salvation. This doctrine we should teach with all assurance, for it is the will of God and the condition of our salvation, as well as the seed and nutriment of the Church, which we are to gather and train for Christ, and present to him as his elect bride in the beauty of holiness, and it is that word of salvation, which the Holy Spirit attests in a peculiar manner, *as was clearly demonstrated during the most successful years in the history of our Church from 1867 to 1871.*"—I have italicised this last sentence, because of its importance to the point under consideration. The period referred to by the Bishops (1867-1871) as "the most successful years in the history of our Church," was a time when there was the greatest earnestness and directness in preaching, writing and working on the special line of holiness. This is in itself a vindication of the "holiness movement" as it was carried on in those years, and it proves the statement, that "the days of our greatest prosperity were those in which we gave the most earnest attention to holiness"—to the spreading of experimental and practical sanctification. I find this same view further confirmed by reports in our Church periodicals of the remarkable success of holiness meetings, held during the prosperous period before mentioned.

In 1871 the editor of our German Monthly—the *Evangelical Magazine*, gave a brief report of such meetings, which reads thus: Recently we visited several camp-meetings on the Chicago District, Illinois Conference, where we witnessed, not only the conversion of sinners, but also saw believers obtain the blessing of entire sanctification, and heard them give clear testimony of this precious grace. We rejoiced most of all to hear the clear distinct and joyful profession of a dear ministerial brother, with whom we spent our youthful years in the Gospel ministry on new and hard Western fields; whom we also know to be one of our most active and self-sacrificing preachers, having served successfully for a number of years as Presiding Elder. However, for several years past he could not just agree with the so-called holiness movement; but now, having an experience in his own heart, which he obtained at one of these meetings (holiness meetings), he has come into the light, and is clearly and decidedly for the cause, the "movement;" and, it seems to us, also for the so-called new measures.

> This profession made a powerful impression upon *many*. The immediate effects were most blessed, and will certainty produce unspeakable results for eternity. From this circumstance we are led to the following observations:
>
> 1. To the upright God will give light. Whoever desires, with all his heart, only that which is well pleasing to God, will be guided by the Holy Spirit into all truth, and, consequently to the right point.
>
> 2. In the matter of our saving religion we come into the true light and into certainty, only by a heart experience. What the clearest mind cannot master through the keenest disquisition, is satisfactorily solved by the child-like faith of the simple heart that seeks after light, purity, and Christ likeness. God gives assurance to the heart, and when once the heart is assured, when it once rests in the great peace which Jesus gives to those who live only in him and for him, then will also the head be correct.
>
> 3. Oh, the unspeakable responsibility connected with the Gospel ministry! We often heard the brother above

named preach powerfully on full deliverance from all sin—a perfect salvation, but we never saw nor realized that deep, powerful impression, which was made by his testimony, at the close of his sermon. A minister may preach full deliverance from all sin through Christ, but as long as he has not experienced this deliverance himself he is hindered and crippled, no matter how earnest he may be. And such a one either does not believe from his heart what he teaches, or he does not live according to what he believes. He that believes in his heart what he teaches, and lives according to his belief, will certainly realize the effect of his faith in himself. How much more useful such a person can be!

IV
THE VOICE OF TESTIMONY

"YE ARE MY WITNESSES"

A CHRISTIAN'S EXPERIENCE of salvation and of the wonderful ways of God is a treasure which he must not hide away where it will neither glorify God, nor do others any good; for Christians are the body of Christ and members one of another. "All are yours;" and this "all" includes also every Christian's experience. And God does not unfrequently so shape one's Christian career that it may become a help to others. Job's severe trial was not permitted on his account, for God himself testified that there was "none like him in the earth, a perfect and an upright man, one that feareth God, and escheweth evil," but he was tried so severely that he might be an example of patience and of Divine deliverance to all coming generations. "Behold we count them happy which endure. *Ye have heard of the patience of Job, and have seen the end of the Lord, that the Lord is very pitiful and of tender mercy.*" James 5. 11. Indeed the Bible is full of this truth.

But no one's experience can be a perfect guide to another, for God leads differently and "works in us both to will and to do *according to his good pleasure."* Different callings require different leadings. Essentially all Christian experience is the same, for it is wrought by the same Spirit, who leads all souls to the same Christ, who is made unto all alike "wisdom, righteousness, sanctification and redemption;" but circumstantially it differs more or less in all.

With these well chosen words from the pen of R. Yeakel, the reader is introduced to one of the most important divisions of this book. In the great work of salvation, *teaching* and *testimony* must go hand in hand. No theory can be of any value unless its truth can be demonstrated. Neither would our most exact theological statements or teachings, in reference to justification, regeneration, and sanctification, be of any value to men if the principles which they enunciate were never known to enter into individual human experience. But, thank God, there has always been "a cloud of witnesses" to the truth of Christ's ability and willingness to save. These are they, who, upon hearing "the form of sound words," can say. *"We know"* — we have "tasted and seen" — "the Lord *hath done great things for us,* whereof we are glad." To a few of these voices our attention is here invited.

Experience of Rev. J. P. Leib

This faithful veteran of the old mother conference, who fell asleep in Jesus, Sept. 7, 1875, after nearly half a century of successful ministerial work, in the Church of his choice, made the following public confession at a camp-meeting, on Milford circuit, shortly before his death:

"I, John P. Leib, at the age of 72 years, and after having served the Lord 51 years, and preached the Gospel 45 years, confess to-day, openly and in the presence of you all, that I have found remission of sins, and redemption in the blood of the Lamb, and that I am consecrated to the Lord with all that I am and have, for time and eternity! Amen."

EXPERIENCE OF SAVILLA KRING

This talented young sister (now the wife of Rev. C. C. Poling), who for several years past has been doing very effectual evangelistic work in various parts of the Church, after being earnestly solicited to give her testimony a place among these voices, has written the following glowing account of her experience:

> "The mercy of the Lord is from everlasting to everlasting upon them that fear Him, and His righteousness unto children's children."
>
> This language came very forcibly to my mind, and my full heart was made to overflow with praise to God for his manifold kindness to one of the least of his little ones, even me, as I was standing in the shadow of a tree, near my grandfather's (Rev. John Stull's) old homestead, among the mountains of Western Pennsylvania. The green fields along the slope of the Laurel Hill were a feast to the eye. From the top of the hill might have been seen the blue line of the Alleghanies, but for a time these were forgotten, and while the sun was kissing the tree-tops, and smiling upon the meadows, I knelt upon the verdant carpet, and with folded hands and heart uplifted, while tears of gratitude freely flowed, I listened. The stillness of the early morn seemed broken with a voice from the "everlasting hills," reechoing the history of early life in the "Evangelical Association," as experienced by my forefathers, and repeated to me here when I was but a little child. The whispering of the breeze among the branches clothed in richest robes of Autumn or never-fading green, and the music of the water flowing over the pebbles in the

brook, brought back to me the prayers and hymns which greeted my ears while with the dearest ones on earth I met in family devotion, in earliest days. Oh, memory's buds, how fragrant still with Christian counsel, and the prayers of parents who taught their "little girls" the Bible way of life! My soul doth magnify the Lord, first, for His own most precious love which brought salvation near me, and next, for praying, Christian parents.

I cannot remember of a time when I did not love God and desire to be a Christian. While I was yet quite young my parents left Pennsylvania and moved to Columbiana Co., Ohio, where we lived for nearly two years with our much beloved, now sainted Bishop Long. During this time, my older sister, Priscilla, now the wife of Rev. C. C. Beyrer, of the Indiana Conference, was converted. This made a deep impression upon my mind, and I determined also to seek "a new heart." Not long after her conversion my parents felt it their duty to join my now aged grandparents in their new home in Western Ohio. Here we had no church privileges, and it was a source of great regret to us all. "This will not do," said my grandfather, and so one of his barns was set in order, and our ministers, who preached occasionally some distance from us, were prevailed upon to come and hold a meeting. Here, after surmounting the difficulties and opposition similar to those so familiar to all who have come out from the world and united their interests with Christ, I was most gloriously converted, beyond the possibility of a doubt. I *knew* it. The Spirit of God bore witness with my spirit that I was "the child of a King." The very earth seemed changed. "Old things had passed away, and all things had become new." Once "dead," but now "alive." Hallelujah! A class was organized, and I at once felt it my duty to participate in the various services.

Not only was I conscious of this being my duty, but it was to me a gracious privilege and pleasure. I had a burning desire for the salvation of souls. My unconverted schoolmates were lying heavily upon my heart, and I was frequently impelled to converse with them personally upon the subject so dear to me. At times, however, I found my natural timidity hindering me. Being young in years and experience, I was often restrained. I was enabled to pray in their presence, and for them, without much embarrassment, but when called upon to testify to the goodness of God and his manifestations of love to me, an unaccountable trembling would seize me, and I would stand confused, bewildered, almost speechless. Some time after my conversion we removed to the town of Van Wert, close by. Here, for the first time in my life, my dear sister and I had the privilege of a real church home in the Evangelical Association. But with new privileges came new responsibilities. Sister was elected Sunday-school superintendent and class-leader, and I was expected to take a prominent part in the work. Praise the Lord! with new responsibilities came "grace sufficient." But, much to my sorrow, I was still vexed with a man-fearing spirit. I continued at school; and now I found within me remains or uprisings of envy, though by prayer and faith I was enabled to keep them from being exposed to view. It is an undeniable truth that when a member of the class would arise to occupy a seat above myself it would occasion unpleasantness within me. I had not learned "in honor to prefer another." Here, again, occurred a marked change in my experience. We were again denied the privilege of a church home, through circumstances that I need not mention here.

 My father being a presiding elder in the Pittsburgh Conference, was obliged to be absent from home most of the time. Mother was in delicate health, and sister Priscilla married and gone to labor in the Lord's vineyard with her husband. May was still very young. Everything seemed to have taken a turn. The majority of my companions were professing Christians —popular and gay. There was no end to "innocent amusement," and, being naturally of a jovial, fun-loving disposition, and always cautious and fearful lest I should offend, I found myself wanting to be "with the crowd." These thoughts would be presented: "If you never comply with their requests, nor accept their invitations, you will merit their displeasure and drive them from you. Show yourself sociable, retain their friendship, and win to Jesus those still unsaved. By going with them this will be accomplished." Here was revealed to me a man-pleasing spirit and love of the world. Permit me to say, to the glory of God, that all this time I never neglected a known duty, or *willfully* committed a wrong act. I had an incessant thirst and indescribable longing for more spiritual knowledge and Divine light. My concern for souls was constantly intensifying. My health now failed, and I was obliged to quit my studies. I was employed as teacher in a school some distance from our little city. The memories of those walks, from my boarding-place to the school-house, will ever be among the sweet things of my life. The Bible was my "treasure-box." The morning was all glorious with the presence of Jesus. "Under His wing" I rested at noonday. The night was light with the brightness of His countenance. I was happy, oh, so happy, all the time, but not just satisfied. Many sacred moments swiftly fled as I knelt in a quiet nook, with the stars shining above me, or the moon shedding her soft, mellow light about me as I whispered, "Thanks, dearest Father, for what Thou hast *done*, and art *doing*; but oh, for precious Jesus' sake, fill this void. Oh, give me something, I know not what it is; but conscious I am that I need a *distinct something*." I was frequently so filled with the joy of salvation that I did not care for the "bread which perisheth," and at times too happy to sleep after retiring at night; and still I wanted *that "something."*

Praying for Holiness

I never had heard a sermon on the doctrine of holiness, and did not understand it, else I would have known what the "something" was for which I was praying. Father had often spoken of the efficacy of the blood, and of the power of God to save, not only from the *guilt* of sin, but from the *love* of it as well. Sister had tried to explain to me how, by an *act* of faith, the heart is *cleansed*, and, by a *constant trust, kept* clean. Books and periodicals upon the subject graced the library, but it still seemed veiled to me. My daily prayer was: "Lord, lead me; teach me!" In the providence of God I was now led to the Friend's or Quaker church. I cannot describe my feelings, as, from time to time, on my return home from my school, I found my way to this shining temple. I seemed to have gotten back home to the humble little Evangelical church. Testimonies gushing from hearts on fire with the Holy Spirit, were burned into my very soul, and the sermons I listened to there will be repreached to me while I live below; and, when we all get home, I'll not forget again to praise God for those plain Gospel truths. Here let me pause one moment in silence to weep and praise. Now *help* me sing, "Praise God from whom all blessings flow"—again; *again.*

One Sabbath morning, after Bro. Barton Jones had preached, as usual, one of his searching sermons, an opportunity was extended for giving Christian experience. One followed another, in quick succession. I arose and added mine, and just then a ring, glittering on my finger, caught my eye; and at once 1 Cor. 6. 20 flashed upon my mind: "For ye are bought with a price: therefore glorify God in your *body*, and in your spirit, which are God's." None of the Friends had ever said anything to me concerning my attire, but I at once decided that I could very well do without my rings, flowers, and that showy, "foppish" watch chain, and so I laid them off. Here, again, many opposing thoughts were presented, such as these: "Better people than *you* are, wear such things. You will look so odd without them. Your companions will ridicule you," etc. But I was fully conscious that this matter lay between God and *Savilla*; and, with a wistful look at these adornments, I said: "I know; but *I* cannot with a clear conscience continue them, and I *will* not." I received a blessing right there, but it was not that for which I longed. My term of school closed, and I returned home, with poorer health than when I left. I thought my life's journey nearly ended, and, but for my parents and other loved ones, I would have preferred going. I had an intense longing to see God, and at times I earnestly desired to be released from this body, that I might know how to worship Him more perfectly. Time's swift wings had carried me to November, 1876. The Friends were protracting a meeting in their church. The first Sabbath morning of the meeting dawned beautifully, and I went to the house of God with a full heart. Oh, memorable day! In the morning "the tide was already very high," and it continued to rise all day. In the evening people from every direction gathered in, and the house was filled to overflowing. After the sermon an invitation was given, and penitents pressed to the mercy-seat. Being directed to offer encouragement to penitents, I knelt down, and, after a few words of prayer for the mourner, I again went to the Father, saying, "Now please, for dear, *dear* Jesus' sake, *now* supply *my* need!" At any cost? Yes, at *any* cost. Then followed a searching time. This body must be presented a *living* sacrifice in a sense vastly beyond the power of description. I was in the presence of the Most High, sinking lower and lower in humility before Him. Every member was being singled out. These eyes to see for Jesus. That excluded following with them the lines of anything like light literature, or willing looks upon anything that would lead the mind in opposition to His will. These ears to be closed to every vain or vulgar sound—everything intended to lead this mind away from Christ, for the intellect must be wholly his. These feet, willingly to walk in paths where the Father would have me go. This heart to be His royal throne.

I was growing faint with His loveliness, but I whispered, "Yes; yes; yes." That I was not yet quite conscious of the import of these questions was revealed to me when the Master softly asked me, "Will you give your tongue to 'tell it all'?" I was startled, and exclaimed, "Dearest Father, I cannot 'tell it.'" "Will you try?" "Oh, but I am so timid—I am young. If I were a man, I'd try; but I'd be called a 'woman preacher' or an 'evangelist.' Oh, I cannot; my associates would all leave me. I might have to arise before great multitudes. I have not the necessary qualifications, and I could not bear the criticisms. I fear public opinion. All our people, from the Bishop down, would oppose me." It seemed to me I must be dying. I *was* dying to self, and the struggle was severe. "For the sake of perishing souls, will you 'tell it'?" Once more I faintly whispered, "God helping me, I *will*! Once more—oh, has the end not yet come? "Your body, soul, and spirit; your memory, mind, and will; all your days, and all your hours—you have given to God to be used by Him *anywhere, everywhere*?" "Oh, but I cannot leave home! My dear father is far away on Zion's walls, Priscilla in the vineyard with her husband: I cannot leave my dear mother and little sister May. I'll 'tell it,' only let me 'tell it' here." Now Jesus stands before me, a halo of glory encircling Him, His locks wet with the dews from the rugged mountain, where he sought the wanderer. His face, beaming with heavenly radiance, is bruised and stained with tears and blood. His hands are extended, and from the wounds which the nails have made the crimson drops are falling. His feet are bleeding, too, and from his side the blood freely flows. Now one wounded hand upon his thorn-crowned head, the other on his pierced side. One look of loving sympathy, one smile so sweetly sad upon me, then on the world about me. Oh, see! Oh, look a little longer! Hush! he speaks—"For *thee*, for *thine*, I have suffered *all* this. Will you *go* and *tell it*?" "He that loveth father or mother more than me, is not worthy of me." "O my adorable Redeemer," exclaimed my heart, "I love thee more than all else, by thy grace I *will tell it anywhere, everywhere*."—'Tis done—*Glory be to the Father! Glory to the Son! Glory to the Holy Ghost!*—The last "shore line" was cut, and borne upon the billows of His love I floated out, *out* in this boundless, bottomless ocean, still farther away from the rocks and sand-bars. Yea, I had "crossed the Jordan," I was resting upon the bosom of my Saviour, with his arms folded about me, and he whispered into my soul, words of heavenly love. I was inhaling the fragrance of the flowers, and feasting upon the delicious fruits growing near the entrance to "Beulah Land." The sweetness of heaven was flowing over me, and permeating my whole being. I cannot tell how long this season of thus communing with God continued, but when I again opened my eyes to earthly surroundings only "the little company" was present. Tears fell silently from the eyes of smiling ones around me, a "weight of glory" rested upon all. A holy hush pervaded the house. All felt it.

My own soul was too full to speak audibly, but the language was: 'Tis Holiness! 'Tis Perfect Love. This is the "something," thank God, I have it. Now give me *more of it*. More holiness! With heartfelt, "Praise the Lord! Thank God"! whispered around me we left the church, and I was led home. I retired, and with folded arms, and eyes turned heavenward breathed, "At peace, sweet peace." The King was swaying his scepter through every avenue of my soul. My heart was expanding, and every moment brought into it more glory. Morning came and I arose, and looking about me asked, "Where is Savilla"? How small I was, how absolutely nothing. How fitting now the words, "I am crucified with Christ, nevertheless I live, yet not I, but Christ liveth in me, and the life which I now live in the flesh I live by the faith of the Son of God who loved me, and gave himself for me." Oh, can it be! He loved even me. How wonderful! God, the *mighty God, my Father*! Jesus, my real *personal Saviour,* my *brother*! Never before did I so realize my utter nothingness and unworthiness. From that moment to this I have never had the least desire for the gaieties of the world. Since then temptations stronger than ever before have been presented, but never a favorable response from my heart, or an inclination or desire to yield. Trials come, it is true, but always "grace sufficient" to praise God. Tempests have raged without, but the inner calm remained undisturbed. Opposition? Yes, but "if God is for us, who can be against us"? "I know His sheltering wings of love are *always* o'er me spread." I never arise to "tell it" without trembling under the weight of my unworthiness and responsibility, but never from fear of man, be it in the presence of few or thousands, of the learned or the illiterate.

Praise the Lord! "Perfect Love" casteth out fear. I often err in judgment, but of this I am *confident*, "The *blood of Jesus Christ, his Son, cleanseth* ME *from all sin.*" I have been requested to tell my experience, but I cannot. It is untellable. Mute with wonder at God's goodness to me, prostrate before him I lie. Filled with a sense of my unworthiness I hide my face in the dust, and glory not save in the Cross of Christ my Justifier, Jesus my Sanctifier. Again I call upon all within me to praise God for granting my desire, and enabling me by his grace to count all things but loss for the excellency of the knowledge of Christ Jesus my Lord.

I was justified in May 1868, and wholly sanctified in Nov. 1876.

So help me ever, Father, to "worship the Lord in the beauty of holiness." And, unto him that loved us, and washed us from our sins in his own blood; and hath made us kings and priests unto God and his Father, to him be glory and dominion forever and ever. Amen.

Greensburg, O.

EXPERIENCE OF REV. J. BOWERSOX

From the *Living Epistle* of 1870, I quote the following testimony of Rev. J. Bowersox, who for some years past has been a faithful missionary in Oregon. He says:—

Jesus has saved me from all the pollution, as well as guilt of sin. For his glory I will humbly record it.

I was converted from the power of sin and Satan unto God January 19th, 1860. So wonderful was the change, so bright the evidence, that I never could doubt it. My very chamber appeared to be illuminated with the glory of God, while my tongue

> "Could not express
> The sweet comfort and peace
> Of my soul in its earliest love."

Soon after, however, I discovered that my heart was not entirely pure. I had many severe struggles, but hearing old and young tell of similar experiences, I concluded that all Christians had to struggle with inward depravity until, or near unto death. While I believed that entire sanctification was attainable in this life, and aspired to gain all that it is my privilege to enjoy, my ideal of it did not rise higher than to seek it in a general, indefinite way. I sought it too much by works, and therefore did not expect it *now*. This was quite in harmony with the teachings and experience of those around me. Their standard, like my own, was *too low*.

As a minister, I felt increased responsibilities, and the great need of a deep-toned piety, in order to be a pattern and leader of the flock. I strove to rise higher, but, alas! how often and how long did impurity within—which I mistook for temptations from without—disturb my peace, and retard my progress. I often deeply deplored and mourned over my spiritual barrenness and inefficiency. By searching the Scriptures, and reading sacred biography I found I was not under all circumstances what God required me to be, and what others, of similar condition, had become by grace. Upon strict examination I found much within that was not of Christ—self-will, passion, inordinate desires and affections—all kept under by grace, but not cast out. They often caused me to yield, more or less, while I should have remained immovable. Thus my course was irregular, and my joys spasmodic.

I saw that I lived beneath my privilege and duty—that I must be "perfect in love," to fill up my measure of usefulness, and thus bring more glory to Christ. I prayed for heavenly guidance. Light came, and led me to the blood that "cleanseth from all sin." A terrible struggle ensued. I was tempted to quibble and criticise. "Perhaps it is all a delusion," said the tempter, "you are mistaken—you received only a great blessing. You will be thought odd and fanatical." Thus Satan, by persecution and ridicule, sought to destroy my confidence. The I (*self*) died hard.

Before reaching this point, my soul "groaned" for purity, for my conviction of indwelling depravity— not guilt—was as pungent as when I was first awakened. And, blessed be God! in the month of August, 1868, while alone in the grove, wrestling with the Lord, consecrating and reconsecrating myself, my entire all, item by item, with a view to heart-purity and holiness of life, I was enabled to lay hold on the promise, and trust Christ by simple, naked faith, when down came the power, the blood was applied and my heart washed from all pollution. Salvation, like cooling water welled up in my soul, and filled my entire being. My peace was indescribable—my rest in Christ such as I had never before enjoyed. Glory to the Lamb forever and ever! Thus the purification *begun* in my soul, in regeneration, was *now complete*.

The tempter's suggestion "not to confess or preach it," I soon thwarted by telling others what Christ had done for me, and entreating them to seek the same grace at once. I soon found I was most blest when most specific and definite.

I now began to live a moment at a time, walking by faith, and thus, for nearly a year and a half, I have been kept in "perfect peace." Oh, how unworthy of it!

I thank God for this baptism of the Spirit. With it began a new era in my Christian life. I love the Saviour more because of it. His Word is more precious to me, work for him a greater delight, and my communion with him sweeter and more constant. My peace now abides, and flows like a river. I grew in grace before, but since all the "roots of bitterness" are gone, my soul is better prepared for rapid development of the Christian graces. The soul grows faster in such a state. I am not exempt from temptations, but I find a vast difference since no depravity remains within to give sympathy and support to enemies without. Would that I had enjoyed this fulness long ago! I am sure my life would have been more useful, my walk more exemplary, my conversation more chaste, my labors as a pastor more successful in leading sinners to Jesus, and Christians to higher degrees in holiness. These are sad regrets. Up to the time of my *full* acceptance I know of none that I led into *full* salvation, because I could not speak from experience. I myself knew not the better way. But since then I have seen one after another plunge into the fountain, and come out gloriously saved.

Reader, are you pure in heart—*entirely so*? If not, seek to become so without delay. If you are, then join me in ascribing praise unto him that loved me, and washed me "from all my sins in his own precious blood."

Experience of Rev. H.J. Bowman

My Conversion

At the age of fourteen, while attending a camp-meeting on the farm of Joseph Brubaker, in Somerset Co., Pa., the Lord brought me under such deep conviction that I gladly and earnestly set about seeking the pardon of my sins. I felt so sin-sick—so burdened in my soul, that I was willing to do anything for relief. A good kind brother, Rev. Jacob Rank, then our pastor, seeing me in the congregation, at once discovered my trouble, and kindly invited me to the altar of prayer. I did not wait for a second invitation, but instantly consented to go. Upon rising to my feet I found my whole frame shaking, so that it was impossible for me to walk without assistance; but being supported by the dear brother already mentioned, I reached the " Mourner's Bench" all broken up. With cries, and sobs, and tears, I lay there before the Lord for several hours, when instantly my faith took hold upon Christ, and an indescribably sweet sensation of love came into my heart. It thrilled my entire being, and I felt as though I could press all mankind to my bosom if only my arms were long enough. This blessed change was wrought in me about the middle of June, 1849. After returning home from this meeting I at once began a life of prayer—secret prayer. But the devil came very near cheating me out of my first season of prayer in the closet. I had been very careful to select a retired place where I knew no person would see, or disturb me, and yet, the instant my knees touched the floor, I was tempted to think some one was present, staring at me, and before I had time to take a second thought I was upon my feet again. But it was just for a moment, for I suddenly recognized it as a trick of the devil, and at once knelt down again and prayed.

From that day to this I have never given up secret prayer, although, I have to regret it, that at times these prayers have been entirely too formal and destitute of faith.

But while I was prompt and determined in establishing the habit of *secret* prayer, I unfortunately failed at the very beginning, in regard to the duty of *public* prayer. I was naturally very timid. Perhaps no boy was ever more bashful than I, and so I refused to lead in prayer at the first prayer-meeting that I attended after my conversion. This gave the enemy some advantage over me, and I soon lost the delicious sweetness of my experience. The result of this neglect was, that in a few yearn afterwards I was classed among those who were backslidden. Yet, I could hardly consent to be thus considered, simply because I continued to observe my regular hours and places for private devotions. But I finally went to the altar of prayer again, with other penitents, and was graciously restored to the favor of God. From this time forth I took up every Christian duty that presented itself, and found a real enjoyment in active Christian work! Thus I continued for about four years, often feeling wonderfully blest of the Lord.

I do not remember ever hearing a definite sermon, in those days, on the subject of holiness, but my father used to tell of a few persons who had obtained sanctification. One was a dear aunt, a member of the Lutheran church, who, he said, was sanctified at the time she was converted; but which he told me was a very unusual thing. The other was a preacher (Bro. H. Bucks), who had been on our circuit, and had obtained this blessing after a severe struggle, of which he used to speak to father. After all there was a great deal of good preaching at that time, and by it I was led to see that I might and should have a deeper religious experience. Just what I needed, or how to get it, I did not know, but I hungered and thirsted intensely for a richer supply of grace. At last an opportunity was presented which seemed like a special visitation from the Lord to lead me into my long desired experience, but alas! alas! I failed to improve it, and was nearly ruined by

A Wrong Decision

It was during a series of meetings which I attended, that the conviction came to my heart, that I should go to the altar of prayer and seek "a deeper work of grace," or "a fuller assurance of my acceptance with God." The invitation was to sinners, and when I felt as though I should go forward, it was instantly suggested to my mind that such a step would injure the cause of religion. That, inasmuch as I was known to be an active Christian, and had been for a number of years, it would appear, either as if I had been a hypocrite, or had been deceived; and in either case I thought it would only damage the cause. Of course I also felt a man-fearing spirit within me, and that no doubt caused me to decide upon not going forward. But no sooner than I had concluded not to go, the preacher said, "If there is any brother or sister here, desiring a deeper work of grace, or a brighter evidence of Divine acceptance, let such come forward." Again my mind passed through the same struggle, and, although I felt as if the Lord had caused that call to be made specially for me, to my sorrow I again refused; for my timidity led me to follow the devil's reasonings rather than my convictions. But oh, such darkness as this brought upon my soul! I left the Church at the close of that service with a terribly distressed heart, which for several weeks grew worse and worse. And all this because my proud, timid nature shrunk from the thought of revealing my condition to others who might have helped me out. For about three weeks I agonized day and night, in prayer to God, for deliverance, and at the close of that period passed into a state of joyful hope and rest, and for a short time had great satisfaction in my communings with God. But I soon had the same battle to fight over, and with about the same result, only the relief came sooner. From this time on I grew in grace and became more and more established. But as the years passed by I felt that I had sustained a great loss by the wrong decision of that night, when I was so deeply moved to consecrate myself anew to God at the altar of prayer.

The thought of this blunder finally became such a source of annoyance to me, that I was tempted at times to abandon my profession of religion altogether for awhile, and then make a better start.

Meanwhile I had entered the ministry and had the pleasure of seeing many precious souls happily converted through my feeble labors, which it pleased the Lord to make fruitful. To God be all the glory for the successes achieved!

But, through all these years of labor and fruit-gathering, of trial and triumph, with much joy in the Lord, I nevertheless deeply felt that something was lacking in my experience, and I knew not how to have it supplied *after having refused it* as I had done. I had an intense desire to be as deeply pious as God wanted me to be.

And, whenever I would read the lives of holy men and women this desire became still more intensified. I remember no book of this kind that contributed more to these aspirations of my soul than Rev. James. Caughey's "Earnest Christianity."

My Views of Holiness

Concerning the doctrine of Christian Perfection I was always in harmony with the statement of it as contained in our Discipline, and zealously defended it with the Scriptures. Gradually I received light which enabled me to discover my imperfect inner life and the hinderances which were in the way of my complete conformity to Christ, and of my greater usefulness. By this increasing light I was also enabled gradually to consecrate myself more fully to God. One point after another along the line of consecration seemed to become clear to my mind, so that I was led to yield more and more to God. By one peculiar process the Lord led me to consecrate my family, by another my body with all its powers, by another my mental faculties; so that *all my studies* should be directed to the glory of God. With most intense interest did I watch the special efforts that were being made here and there to get believers sanctified. This was particularly so with reference to the work of Mrs. Phoebe Palmer. I read her "Four Years In The Old World." and circulated it among the people of my charge, and sought in this way, as well as by my preaching to awaken an interest on the subject of holiness.

Year after year passed by and sinners were being converted, but I knew of no one that I had ever led into the light and experience of entire sanctification. Finally, while serving in the Iowa Conference as Presiding Elder, one of the preachers on my district sought and obtained this blessing. More than once, that dear young brother sought counsel of me and after telling him all I could about it, he was left to wonder where I stood in reference to the experience of this grace. But he finally outstripped me, and gave me a glowing report of the goodly land into which he had entered. When he told me that he had obtained the blessing of entire sanctification my first thought was, "You poor brother, how do you know that the blessing you received is sanctification?" Afterward I was greatly astonished at having thought thus, because of the interest and faith that I had always had in this work. But it only proved to me that a true understanding of this grace cannot be reached outside of our personal experience of it. Our most luminous theories fall far below the practical experience of this wonderful change. It is rather a strange coincidence that this young brother—Rev. W. H.

Bucks —should be the son of the first preacher that ever professed holiness to my father, as before mentioned.

"Do You Profess Holiness?"

It was not long after Bro. Bucks came into the experience, when a dear sister on my district became greatly concerned about holiness. I had just preached on the subject (at a camp-meeting) and urged the believers to seek this great blessing, and now this sister was hungering and thirsting for it, and this led her to seek more definite instruction. Approaching me on the camp ground, she said "Bro. Bowman, I do want the blessing of holiness."—I replied that I was glad to hear it. "Well," said she, "do you profess holiness?" This was bringing the matter right home to my heart, and I replied in all sincerity, "That is a delicate matter to profess; I know that I have advanced in that direction but it is a delicate matter to profess holiness." "Oh," said she, "I do so much desire it; will you pray for me?" I answered affirmatively; and as I turned away to walk to my tent something within me said, "You promise to pray for an experience in another, which you are not sure that you enjoy yourself!" Then followed a train of reflections as to what a preacher ought to be; and chief among these reflections was the thought that our people have a right to the benefit of *our own experience* in regard to those things which we teach them, and to which we urge them. They are entitled to know how we reached that point in our experience; and if we must inform them that we have not reached it, it both humbles *us* and discourages *them.*

I have often blessed God for that pointed question from Sister E., through which I was so fully convinced that preachers owe it to their people to have the experience of full salvation, in order that they may be enabled to show inquirers the way to its attainment. My convictions and my longings for heart purity were clearer and more intense from this on than ever before; and, it was not very long after this that the light I sought broke in upon my soul in meridian splendor. It was while attending the session of the Board of Publication, at Cleveland, O., in the early part of October, 1870, that this new epoch in my Christian life began. Here (in the Calvary Evangelical Church), for the first time in my life I attended a regular "holiness meeting." I listened to plain directions given by the leader, Bro. J. Young, and was convinced that I had very nearly reached the blessed experience for which my soul was longing. Yet, I was also convinced that something was still lacking. I had *no assurance* that the work had been wrought in me, and I took that as sufficient evidence that I was not yet entirely sanctified. I so stated the matter in that meeting, with the remark, "I believe that I have consecrated myself fully, but I have not yet had faith enough to believe that the Lord has accepted my offering." This drew the attention of the entire audience toward me, and before I was aware of it I was led to where I either had to commit myself as a seeker of holiness, or virtually say I did not just then want it. It seemed very humiliating for me to commit myself in the way I was urged to do it. And, when I was about to consent, a voice rang through my ears, saying; "You, a Presiding Elder, from Iowa, get up here and ask this congregation to pray that you may be entirely sanctified!" But just at that instant I recognized that the call was identical with that which, to my sorrow I had refused nearly sixteen years before, and feeling as though it were my last opportunity I sprang to my feet and stood committed as a seeker of perfect love, with a request "to be prayed for." Then came a struggle. The tempter tried to make me feel ashamed of what I had done. And, to make my case still more perplexing I had promised the pastor, Bro. Sichley, to preach that evening, and had already chosen the following text: "But the God of all grace, who hath called us unto his eternal glory by Christ Jesus, after that we have suffered awhile, make you perfect, stablish, strengthen, settle you." 1 Pet. 5. 10. The difficulty which presented itself here was that my text would lead me to preach on Christian perfection, and I had now exposed myself as one who did not possess what I had prepared to preach unto others.

So I set about the task of finding another text, but all my search was vain. The afternoon passed away, and the hour for preaching came, but still it seemed that from Genesis to Revelation, there was but one text for me, and that was the one already chosen. Seeing that there was no escape from it, I tried, in the name of the Lord, to speak of "the call" and "the glory," but said as little as possible of "the perfection" mentioned in the text, and thus ended that memorable Sabbath-day.

The Fulness Obtained

It was early the next morning (Oct. 10, 1870) when I again turned to this text, in a volume of Clarke's commentary, to see what this learned Divine had to say about it. I read—"*He will make you* perfect"—"put you in *complete joint*, as the timbers of a building," when, instantly, a ray of light darted into my mind, and I could see that my deliverance was near at hand. The view that there opened up to my mental vision was so charming that I was anxious to remember it just as it came, and so I took a pencil and paper to record my passing thoughts. In this state of mind, but without the least excitement, I returned to my bed-chamber to meditate, to pray, and to receive what I confidently believed the Lord was about to bestow upon me.

Kneeling there I wrote the following out line of my reflections on 1 Pet. 5. 10, and of

My Complete Consecration

"Perfect you."—Bring joint to joint as timbers in a building. So my various items of consecration must now be brought together into one, that I may be perfected.

I first learned the principle of general resignation, so that I could commit myself and my family to God's care without worry.—Alas! I had nearly forgotten the struggle that brought me this victory.—Then I learned to consecrate all my intellectual powers to God. This, too, I had almost forgotten. I also learned to consecrate my temporal affairs—my body—all the powers of my soul, and my reputation.

These consecrations were made at different times. They have been scattered through a period of years. Between the different points my struggles have been severe. Now I am summing these all up, and whatever is yet unknown to me I now consecrate... Jesus is helping me to bring these "pieces" together... He is perfecting me... I have now given all to Thee... I will - *n-o-t* take it back. Jesus has accepted all. He *now fully saves me*! Glory to his eternal Name!"

I have indicated some omissions here which simply signify the place of many unwritten struggles which came in between these broken sentences. The turning point was on the little word *not* which I have written as above to indicate the stubbornness with which it consented to be written. It was just at the point where I must decide ever after to be known as a professor of holiness, and a positive advocate of it as a distinct experience, that this little word was to be put in for the purpose of "destroying the bridges behind me," and with a clear understanding that it meant nothing less. I would not suffer my hand to write until my heart said "*not*" then, almost involuntarily my hand wrote it, and instantly the glory came and filled my soul with such rapture as I had never known before.

As a result of this instantaneous effusion of grace, I had such an inward sense of purity and of love as was perfectly wonderful. A few hours after this mighty change was wrought in me, my way led me in company with other brethren in the direction of the meeting of our Board of Missions, in Canada, and it was arranged for us to visit Niagara Falls that day. It was my first view of that great wonder of nature, and was a real delight to me; but the grandeur of the roaring cataract was nothing in comparison with the well of living water that was springing up from my heart, and with almost every breath throwing off a silent hallelujah!"

"Now unto him that is able to do exceeding abundantly above all that we ask or think, according to the power that worketh within us, unto him be glory in the Church by Christ Jesus throughout all ages, world without end. Amen."

I have thus given my experience in detail, not as a model, according to which others must expect to be brought into this grace, but with the hope that it may incite and encourage others to follow the leadings of the blessed Spirit until they know that "the God of all grace" has perfected them.

EXPERIENCE OF REV. W. H. BUCKS

MY CONVERSION

I embraced religion January 23, 1866. Then I experienced that God, for Christ's sake pardoned all my sins, and gave me the witness of his Spirit that I was his adopted child.

Soon after my conversion I perceived that there were

still some roots of carnality—sinful propensities, existing in my heart, and striving for the mastery. I knew if these evils which were continually warring within, were not removed I would not be a fit subject for heaven. I occasionally expressed my feelings publicly, but met with no encouragement. Thus I struggled on betwixt darkness and light for over a year. Then for the first time the *Living Epistle* appeared, and I was aroused *anew* and encouraged by it to seek a pure heart. I wrestled and agonized like Jacob of old, resolved not to cease praying until the blessing was realized. I consecrated all, laying soul, body and spirit upon the altar, and having thus made a *full* and unconditional surrender to God, I said, Lord, here is the sacrifice, accept—consume it. Here a mighty struggle ensued, but by distrusting self and placing an unyielding faith in God's ability and willingness to save to the uttermost I was made to feel the soul-quickening and soul-illuminating influences of the Holy Spirit poured into my heart, so that I felt "unutterably full of glory."

But before I entered into this blessed experience, I found that, like many others, I was seeking to *merit* it instead of *receiving* it as a free gift.

Riding out one day in company with Bro. H. J. Bowman, P. E., now editor of the *Epistle*, I opened my heart to him. Finally I said, "Brother Bowman, I have concluded to go home and not attempt to preach another sermon till I am in possession of full salvation." Bro. B. had the theory (would to God he had had the experience then, as later), and he set me right by saying, "Brother, you want to merit or earn holiness, do you not?" That opened my eyes and showed me my error. But oh, if Bro. B. had known how I panted after *experimental instruction*. The struggle began to be intense. It was life or death with me. Power I *must have* or die in the attempt to receive it. Thank God, the darkest hour was just before the break of day. *Light came, rest came, victory came, power came,* all in one wave. It filled me, surrounded me, penetrated soul, body and spirit. I found myself calmly leaning upon the bosom of Jesus, like a babe nestling in its mother's bosom. I knew not where there was the most glory; in me, around me, above me, or below me. I was in a sea of glory.

Since that time (Aug. 19th, 1869), I have found holiness to be a power in the pulpit. I must, I cannot otherwise, I will not otherwise, than preach a *present, free, full* and *uttermost* salvation. Jesus cleanses even me! "I desire to know nothing among men save Christ and him crucified."

EXPERIENCE OF REV. H.F. KLETZING

Professor H.F. Kletzing, whose experience here follows, is a member of the Faculty in the Northwestern College, at Naperville, Ill. His testimony is given as written by himself, a few years ago. He says:

I have much cause to be thankful to the Lord for a praying mother. From my first recollections I was taught to pray, nor do I know of a time when I did not pray in secret, yet I knew nothing of a changed heart, experimentally, until I was fourteen years of age. I then presented myself at the altar of prayer as a penitent, and soon found peace in believing. My attention was first called to heart-purity by my mother. She was a careful reader of *The Guide to Holiness,* and, now, when past recollections crowd upon my mind, I recall the many precious seasons spent in reading to her, or listening while she read the *Guide.* My mind could not always grasp the precious thoughts, but it was food for mother. She was a firm believer in heart-purity, but had not yet attained to the experience. Soon after conversion, I realized the need of a more thorough cleansing, and began to search after truth and light. The Bible and the *Epistle* were the chief sources from which I learned that this great salvation was full and free to all. I saw it was for *me*. Each succeeding number of the *Epistle* showed me the way more clearly, and increased my desire for the fulness in Christ, for, as I received more light, I felt the need of it the more. I knew I was a child of God, for I had the witness of the Spirit and enjoyed many precious seasons, but still I had not complete victory over sin, for I often found roots of bitterness, which caused me much anxiety and many tears. But what joy the blessed word brought me in showing me that there was an all-sufficiency in the Blood of Christ to cleanse and purify my poor heart and make it "even whiter than snow." Like too many others, I longed in vain, not being willing to act. It was not my privilege then, to hear many sermons on the subject, as it subsequently has been. Too many ministers were of the opinion of the brother who thought that "it's a delicate thing to handle," and so left us hungering and thirsting for what we knew it was our privilege to possess. It was not through the teaching of a minister, but of a class-leader, who was conducting a series of meetings, that I was first led to act. I was greatly profited by encouraging words received from our presiding elder, now the editor of the *Epistle*. I tried to make myself better, and, failing in this, made, as I thought, a complete surrender of all to Christ; but instead of finding rest the agony of my soul increased. I soon found by the light of the Spirit that my consecration was defective. I was still cherishing that in my heart which must be given up. Finding no peace, and knowing the hindering cause, I yielded and made a full consecration to God. I found it a great help to write out my consecration, which included time, talents, influence, reputation, memory, mind and everything else for which I am held accountable. To write, "Lord, I give it all to thee *now*" was comparatively easy, but, after counting the cost, "*forever*" was added. Doing this, I considered myself no longer my own, but Christ's property, to *do*, *be* or *suffer* whatever he might see fit. 'Twas then that the refining fire came, and the cleansing blood being applied to my heart, I was saved, wonderfully and completely saved through Jesus' blood. Although there was spiritual growth prior, and there has been subsequent to this "baptism of power," I did not grow into this blessed experience, but received it by a special act of faith in the cleansing power of the blood. I claim no merits of my own, for "I am crucified with Christ," and am continually reckoning myself "dead indeed unto sin and alive unto God." I feel myself quite safe, just as long as I keep trusting fully in Christ, for I very well know that it is only by a momentary act of faith in the atoning blood that I am kept. Yes, "kept by the power of God through faith." The peace of Christ fills my soul, my blessed Saviour is my constant companion, and a sharer with me in all my plans. I have realized the truth of the poet's words:

"The fountain of delight unknown,
   No longer sinks beneath the brim,
But overflows and pours me down,
   A living and life-giving stream."

I am peacefully resting and trusting in Jesus, having no fears for the future, but leaving all to Him, who careth even for the sparrow. I am cheered by the thought that, if I trust Him, He will "guide me with his eye." When I think of all that the Lord has done for me, I feel like praising him with my whole heart; but realizing the wondrous fulness in store for me, and knowing that there's "still more to follow," my lips fail to express the language of my heart, for it seems amazingly wonderful that even I may be a partaker of such rich gifts! Hallelujah!

EXPERIENCE OF REV. M. KRUEGER

The following testimony, to a "personal experience of entire sanctification," from the pen of Bro. Krueger, a Presiding Elder of the Indiana Conference, was sent to the editor of the *Epistle*, under date of October 18, 1882, to be published either in that Monthly, "or where it is thought proper to use it." I therefore take the liberty to give it a place among these voices, as one of the most distinct testimonies concerning this blessed experience. Hear what he says:

> I was gloriously converted to God in the month of March, 1852, at Newburg, Ind. Soon afterward I joined the Evangelical Association, where I found an excellent Church-home. In June, 1856, 1 was licensed to preach, and sent to northern Indiana. For many years I felt that I should be wholly consecrated to God, but when I read the experiences of those who professed to be wholly sanctified, I often thought it was rather an easy way to obtain this blessing by simple faith in God's word, and that they had perhaps backslidden, and were now only reclaimed, and had no further blessing than Christians usually possess. The work appeared to me too superficial to be substantial.
>
> It was after having listened to some powerful and stirring sermons, preached by Bishop J. J. Esher on holiness, that I also attempted to preach on this subject, but I soon found that I was not very well qualified to do so. A good brother, however, who enjoyed the blessing, encouraged me to go on, saying, "Your theory is correct, only you ought to say that you possess it." This I could not do. But I encouraged the people to seek the

blessing, hoping I might thus receive deeper convictions for it in my own heart.

At last I gave myself wholly to God, to be led by Him, according to his will, and to have all sinful lusts and desires taken out of my heart, and that I might be washed "whiter than snow." I let go of everything, and trusted only in *this* word of the Lord—"The blood of Jesus Christ, his Son, cleanseth *me* from all sin." I said nothing for awhile, but soon realized a sweet and abiding rest, peace, and joy, filling my soul. My eyes were bathed—at times even streaming with tears: I could not tell why.

For some time after this, it was a real, holy delight for me to preach this doctrine, and definitely urge believers to seek a clean heart. But after a few years I got off the track, in a measure, because I thought that some of our people did not understand the doctrine, while others feared it was leading to fanaticism. I ceased to speak so definitely about sanctification. Thus I drifted back somewhat into the wilderness, and it became burdensome for me to advocate this holy doctrine. But I again examined my heart closely, and anew consecrated my all to God, and now I can say that Jesus is my satisfying portion. It was while the people were singing:

"I am so wondrously saved from sin,
 Jesus so sweetly abides within"—

that my heart, filled with glory, cried out, "Amen!"

And, now, for a number of years past, the Lord has helped me to walk in this light, and this very moment I know that the precious blood cleanseth me from all sin. I have had greater trials during these years than ever before, but glory to God, his "grace is sufficient!" Oh, if I only had received this wonderful blessing before I started out in the ministry; how much more good I might have accomplished!

Experience of Rev. S. Dickover

The precious experience of this dear brother, with whom I have had a long and pleasant acquaintance, was published in the *Epistle* in 1871, in the form of a letter which I here give entire:

CHICAGO, ILL., June 14, 1871

Dear brother ————, Last night I returned from Deer Grove camp-meeting, and I praise God, that I was there. There I experienced that which I shall not forget throughout eternity. Bless the Lord! Shall I tell you what took place? Twenty years ago when I traveled on Cedar Creek circuit, I realized something similar. Oh. now the Lord did at that time bless me and my feeble labors! During that year over two hundred souls were converted, and I lived at the time entirely in God, and for God. But, alas, I did not remain in that state of grace, though I tried to follow the Lord as a minister of the Gospel, and he still blessed my labors. Since the *Living Epistle* has been published, and there has been so much preaching on the subject of holiness, I have prayed a great deal for the grace of perfect love. Yet I criticised the measures which have been adopted, very much, and believed that much humbug was connected with the National camp-meetings, etc. At our conference session I believed I had experienced the same grace that my brethren confessed as a distinct work. I was sincere in my opinions, but bless God that I went to this camp-meeting. On Saturday evening I obtained a glorious victory. On Sunday afternoon Bishop J.J. Esher preached an old-fashioned evangelical sermon, accompanied with such victorious power as I have not heard from him since he is bishop, and thus one sermon followed the other. Yesterday morning I was to preach once more. I went into the woods to meditate and pray. Oh, how I felt my poverty and entire nothingness! I intended to preach on the prophetic office of Christ. There my heart melted. I made an entire surrender to the Great Teacher, and presented to him an entire sacrifice. Suddenly a stream of light and power came upon me, and penetrated my whole being, so that I trembled and became quite weak in my body. Tears of joy coursed down my cheeks. I could scarcely reach the camp ground. The brethren had been waiting and knew not what it meant that I stayed away so long; and when at last I came it was impossible for me to preach. I stood up and wept and glorified God. I then related my experience as best I could, and encouraged others to seek sanctification. It was enough, the Lord himself preached. There is a great fire burning in Deer Grove. In the evening I took the cars to go home. My heart was so full that I was overcome with weeping. At the depot, and on the way home, the people looked at me, and probably thought that one of my relatives had died.

At 7 P.M. I reached home and went straightway into the prayer-meeting, and there I could not remain silent. I had to tell what the Lord had done for me. Then the fire commenced to burn, and such a prayer- meeting we have never had since I am in Chicago. Dear brother, I can not express my feelings. I could scarcely sleep last night, and to-day the divine power fills my heart, and tears flow almost continually. Hallelujah! Dear brother, I never knew my Saviour as I know him now, and never did I love him so much. Oh, how great, rich, and glorious he is! Oh, what a fulness of love and grace is in him! Bless the Lord to all eternity for what he has done for me!

I am so blest, that I cannot praise my Saviour sufficiently for what he has done for me.

Experience of Mrs. Lizzie Yetley

In the Winter of 1868 and 1869 my mind was first directed to the subject of *present, personal* holiness, through the private correspondence of a dear brother who had recently attained to this blessed experience. I at once became deeply convicted of the great necessity of seeking this blessing. I felt it to be a duty as well as a privilege to be holy. The method of living as so many professed Christians do was not satisfactory to me. I availed myself of all the helps that I could obtain, without mentioning the subject to any one, save this brother. I would take my Bible, get down upon knees, and ask God for light and instruction. I derived much help, strength, and comfort from this. Oh, how I longed for a sermon on holiness! Up to that time I had not heard a definite holiness sermon, had heard no one profess the blessing, had never been urged nor invited to seek the blessing *now*. I knew that God was a just and consistent Being, and that he would require no impossibilities; that he would not require his people to be holy and then leave them to grope their way in the dark. I knew that this requirement implied a promise, and he was oath-bound to keep it. Neither did I doubt his ability or willingness. I consecrated *all* to God, the known and the unknown, *all* to be the Lord's for time and eternity. I prayed, I wrestled, I pruned, lopping off this and that branch which I felt to be in the way. I worked hard; still I did not obtain the desire of my heart. Self was in the way. Self dies hard. Not until I made an *unconditional* surrender of *self* to God, and let him do the work, was I blessed. But oh, how quickly the work was then done!

It was in the month of August, 1869, while seated on a camp-ground, listening to a sermon on holiness, that light broke in upon my soul and my faith claimed the blessing mine. The time, place, and circumstances I shall never forget. My heart cried out:

"I am Thine, O Christ!
　Henceforth entirely Thine
And from this glad hour
　New life is mine.

"No earthly joy can lure
　My quiet soul from Thee
This deep delight so pure
　Is heaven to me."

The reader may ask, What was your evidence.

1. I consecrated all to God, and knew that by his grace I had complied with his conditions of salvation.

2. I believed that the blood of Jesus had power to cleanse from all sin, and that it cleansed *me*; and faith has its own witness. Having consecrated all and believed, I knew that I had done so, and to believe otherwise would be believing contrary to facts, which in this case was impossible; hence faith had its own evidence.

3. When I believed, the Holy Spirit applied the blood of Christ to my heart, of which I was aware, having claimed it, and God's Spirit witnessed with mine that the work was done. I knew for myself that I was made "whiter than snow."

Precious experience! Glorious salvation! Hallelujah!

V
CONCLUSION

"Thus saith the Lord, Stand ye in the ways, and see, and ask for the old paths, where is the good way, and walk therein, and ye shall find rest for your souls." Jer. 6. 16.

THE "OLD PATHS" and the "good way" in which we are to walk have been plainly set before us in this book, and over a hundred voices have been heard calling us to come and walk therein. It is the way of *holiness,* the only way that leads to "the rest that remaineth to the people of God." To this, every voice that has been heard agrees.

When I say "over a hundred voices," I count over *thirty* that have been introduced to the reader *personally* in this book; then I count *sixty-six* others who joined in a *unanimous* vote for the General Conference Resolutions of 1867; and, besides these the Discipline, the Catechism, and the Hymn-Book, to say nothing of all the sainted fathers who adopted the original edition of the Discipline with its present holiness teachings; and last, but not least, the numerous passages of Scripture in which the voice of God is heard directly, all these I count as so many voices united to proclaim this one central truth of the Bible that *only the pure in heart shall see God, and that we may and must be made pure in this life.*

From the Bible and from the church literature, from the ministry and from the laity, from the dead and from the living, these voices have spoken to us, and they all call upon us to secure holiness as a personal experience, and also to assist in spreading it all over these lands.

And now my task is done; and as I leave this volume in the hands of the reader, I pray that every soul that shall ever peruse its pages may *hear* and *heed* that "*still small voice*" which wakes the slumbering soul to lead it to the purifying waters of the fountain of life; and may we all, with those whose voices have here spoken, be permitted finally to sing: "Unto him that loved us, and washed us from our sins in his own blood, and hath made us kings and priests unto God and his Father; to him be glory and dominion forever and ever, Amen."

THE END

Members of Schmul's Wesleyan Book Club buy these outstanding books at 40% off the retail price.

Join Schmul's Wesleyan Book Club by calling toll-free:
800-S₇P₇B₂O₆O₆K₅S₇
Put a discount Christian bookstore in your own mailbox.

Visit us on the Internet at
www.wesleyanbooks.com

You may also order direct from the publisher by writing:
Schmul Publishing Company
PO Box 776
Nicholasville, KY 40340

www.ingramcontent.com/pod-product-compliance
Lightning Source LLC
Chambersburg PA
CBHW060507090426
42735CB00011B/2132